HOPE
FOR CHILDREN
IN POVERTY

HOPE
FOR CHILDREN
IN POVERTY
profiles and possibilities

**Edited by Ronald J. Sider
and Heidi Unruh**

**Foreword by
Marian Wright Edelman**

JUDSON PRESS
PUBLISHERS SINCE 1824
VALLEY FORGE, PA

Hope for Children in Poverty: Profiles and Possibilities

The editors and Judson Press have made every effort to trace the ownership of all quotes. In the event of a question arising from the use of a quote, we regret any error made and will be pleased to make the necessary correction in future printings and editions of this book.

Unless otherwise indicated, Bible quotations in this volume are from the New Revised Standard Version of the Bible, copyright © 1989 by the Division of Christian Education of the National Council of the Churches of Christ in the United States of America. Used by permission. All rights reserved.

Other Bible quotations are from HOLY BIBLE: *New International Version,* copyright © 1973, 1978, 1984. Used by permission of Zondervan Bible Publishers (NIV).

Library of Congress Cataloging-in-Publication Data
Hope for children in poverty: profiles and possibilities / edited by Ronald J. Sider and Heidi Unruh; foreword by Marian Wright Edelman.
p. cm.
ISBN 978-0-8170-1505-3 (pbk. : alk. paper) 1. Poverty—Religious aspects—Christianity. 2. Poverty—United States. 3. Poor children—United States. 4. Adolescence—United States. I. Sider, Ronald J. II. Unruh, Heidi.
BV4647.P6H67 2007
261.8'325—dc22

2007005773

Printed on recycled paper in the U.S.A.
First Edition, 2007.

Tyiya, age 8

CONTENTS

117374

CONTENTS

CONTENTS

CONTENTS

PRAYERS, POEMS, AND SONGS

FOREWORD
Setting Our Moral Compass

More than forty years ago, President Lyndon Johnson declared a War on Poverty and committed people in the United States to a campaign against economic deprivation. Initially, poverty rates did fall. But our nation didn't stay the course, and we haven't won the war. Today 37 million Americans, including nearly 13 million children, still live in poverty.[1] This number is morally and practically intolerable in the richest country in the world.

Who are the nation's poor children? Meet a few of the families who are standing patiently in line one morning at the Smith Chapel Food Pantry in Logan, Ohio. Tonda Sue is a working mom with one child. Her income from babysitting other children doesn't stretch very far, so she has to turn to the food pantry twice a month to make sure her daughter gets enough to eat. Nearby, little Cody, just eighteen months old, waits in line with his mother, Cheryl. Although Cheryl has a new, full-time job as a waitress at the Colonial Inn and receives some child support from Cody's father, she and her toddler still have to stand in the food line to get through the month. Faye's husband drives all the way to Columbus for work, but his income and the $126 a month in food stamps they receive isn't enough to keep their three children fed for the month, so Faye, like the others, gets up early to come to the food pantry.

When the Smith Chapel Food Pantry first opened its doors, it distributed food to 17 families. Five years later, they were serving 560 families, about 1,400 people, every month. Although the twice monthly food distribution doesn't start until 8:30 a.m., on the day of this visit, cars filled with hungry and hopeful children and adults started lining up at 6:00 a.m. Three and a half hours later, the pantry had given away 18 tons of food. Lisa, another mother standing in line near Faye, pointed out, "Last year the food pantry wasn't so packed." But lately, she continued, "people are hungry. They don't have ways to support their families. Jobs are hard to find." It's a scene and a sentiment that's being repeated in small towns and big cities all across our country.

Many people think of poverty simply in terms of inadequate income. But poverty isn't just about income; it represents a constellation of needs, including lack of health insurance, inadequate education, and poor nutrition and housing. Poverty puts children at an unfair disadvantage for many present and future opportunities.

Children who are poor are more likely to die in infancy, have a low birth weight, and experience developmental and health problems. Poor families often are forced to make choices between paying rent and buying food or medicine. One recent report, based on the findings of pediatric health professionals, looked at the cost of food insecurity to young children's health, growth, and development.[2] It concluded that children raised in food-insecure households, such as some of the families relying on the food pantry, are more likely to suffer poor health, including illnesses severe enough to require hospitalization. The average total cost for a single hospitalization for pediatric illness is $11,300. The same amount would purchase almost five years of food stamps for a family receiving the fiscal year 2004 average monthly household benefit of $200.

Poor and minority children face a disproportionate number of risks and disadvantages that often pull them into a "Cradle to Prison Pipeline."® As these risk factors converge to reduce the odds that they will grow up to become productive adults, this pipeline leads children to marginalized lives and premature deaths. Research links poverty to increased likelihood of maltreatment, academic failure, delinquency, and violence.[3] Poverty is the largest predictor of child abuse and neglect; children in families with annual incomes below $15,000 are twenty-two times as likely to be abused or neglected than are children in families with annual incomes of $30,000 or more.[4]

Even mild undernourishment impairs a child's cognitive function, and fourth graders in U.S. public elementary schools with the highest poverty levels have significantly lower reading scores compared with their more affluent counterparts. The Children's Defense Fund estimates that each year that we allow nearly 13 million children to live in poverty will cost our society over $130 billion in future economic output as poor children grow up to be less productive and effective workers.[5] The numbers add up to an inescapable conclusion: Child poverty takes a huge economic toll on our nation, and all Americans pay the price—a price that is far higher than the cost of eradicating poverty.

Protecting the well-being of our children is a basic obligation that adults must embrace and public policies must promote. Failing to do so has both human and social consequences. While all have a stake in improving the lives of the nation's children, for people of faith this is more than just an opportunity: it is a mandate and a calling.

My father was a Baptist preacher, and my mother was a church and community leader. They taught me early on that service is the rent each of us pays for living—it is the purpose of life, not something you do in your spare time. In many communities, churches and other religious congregations are already on the front lines organizing food pantries, collecting donated clothing and goods, and providing other services that help poor children and families. We were reminded of this after Hurricane Katrina, when so many faith leaders reached out to provide shelter and food and clothing and other supports to the storm's victims. Thank God for all the people of faith who are already meeting the most immediate needs of children and families, both in times of crisis and every day.

But our responsibility is not fulfilled by charity alone. Something is deeply wrong in our nation when hard-working parents and their children cannot count on jobs that will pay enough to make ends meet, when they cannot obtain health care for their children, when they cannot rely on a safety net for security during economic downturns, and when they must wake up in the early morning, pile into a car, and spend hours in line hoping for a handout to feed their children.

While people of faith continue to serve with compassion, we also must put our faith into action by speaking out and demanding justice for poor children and families with urgency and persistence. We are living at an incredible moral moment. What people of faith stand for now—and encourage our political leaders to stand for—will shape our nation's and children's futures for decades to come. If ever there was a time for people of faith to stand up and speak up together for justice for children and the poor, it is now.

The test of the morality of a society is how it treats its children. The Unites States is failing that test each day it permits a child to be neglected or abused every 35 seconds; to be born into poverty every 36 seconds; to be born without health insurance every 46 seconds; and to die from gun violence almost every 3 hours.[6] Children are the poorest age group in the country, and millions of children suffer hunger, homelessness, and illiteracy in the richest nation on earth. These facts are not acts of God. They are our moral and political choices as a people. We can and must change them by building together a mighty and unified faith witness and transforming movement for more just choices in our nation—choices that protect and place our children first.

Those of us who believe it is time to close the growing gap between rich and poor and to stop the epidemic of child poverty, who believe our nation should not allow 9 million children to grow up without health insurance, who believe it is wrong to give tax cuts to millionaires and billionaires while imposing budget cuts and caps on children and the poor, and who are concerned about policies that erode the already inadequate and frayed safety net for the vulnerable—we all must come together and join our voices in a mighty chorus crying out and acting for justice.

Poor children present the United States with an opportunity to heed God's call to protect the poor, the orphan, the widow, and the vulnerable. Children are transforming agents in our fractured nation and world. Abraham, Moses, Jesus and his mother Mary, Harriet Tubman, Sojourner Truth, Mary McLeod Bethune, Nelson Mandela, Martin Luther King Jr., and the children in the food line at Smith Chapel all share one thing in common. They, like each of us, entered the world as a baby—God's gift of life, hope, love, and a messenger to the future. Our Creator sent babies in an infinite variety of hues, sizes, shapes, places, and talents—each precious.

Dare we longer mistreat, neglect, abuse, kill, and deny health care to a single child? Dare we value one over another, or hold little ones responsible for unwise adult choices over which the children had no control? Dare the richest nation on earth—blessed to be a blessing—maintain an unjust, morally warped playing field for children and wantonly continue to widen the gap between the haves and the have nots? Dare the people of God stand mute and indifferent?

It's time to reset our nation's moral compass. In 1968, in his last Sunday sermon at Washington National Cathedral, Dr. King recounted the parable of Dives and Lazarus:

> A man went to hell because he didn't see the poor. His name was Dives. He was a rich man. And there was a man by the name of Lazarus who was a poor man, but not only was he poor, he was sick. . . . But he managed to get to the gate of Dives every day, wanting just to have the crumbs that would fall from his table. And Dives did nothing about it. And the parable ends saying, 'Dives went to hell.' . . .
>
> Dives didn't go to hell because he was rich; Dives didn't realize that his wealth was his opportunity . . . to bridge the gulf that separated him from his brother, Lazarus. . . . He never really saw him. He went to hell because he allowed his brother to become invisible. . . . He sought to be a conscientious objector in the war against poverty.
>
> And this could happen to America, the richest nation in the world. . . . There is nothing new about poverty. What is new is that we now have the techniques and the resources to get rid of poverty. The real question is whether we have the will!

Dr. King's warning about the nation's will to see and help its poorest and most vulnerable is the defining question of our time. How will you answer the question posed by 13 million poor and 9 million uninsured children? How will you use your voice, your vote, and your congregational, professional, and personal time and resources to build the transforming movement our children need to live and learn and thrive and embrace the future with hope?

Let me end, as I often like to do, with a prayer:

Prayer of Intercession for Children[7]

For the millions of children who are living in poverty, that despite our society's rejection and inaction, they might know they are loved and valuable in your sight.

For our nation, that we are moved from tolerance of child poverty to passionate work for justice.

For the parents who struggle each day to provide food, pay the rent, keep their families together, and just survive, that they might find community supports that enable them to nurture, enjoy, and spend time with their children.

For the children whose needs are unmet, whose cries go unheard, and whose lives hold little joy, that we might fill their needs, respond to their pain, and seek to enrich their lives.

For the children who are born too soon or too small, that they will receive the special care that they need, and that our nation will learn from their pain to invest adequately in prenatal care.

For the children who are sick and for their parents who don't know how they can pay the bills, that they find care and healing and their parents respite from worry.

For our nation's leaders, that they might make children the nation's highest priority, and fulfill the promises that they make to the children.

For ourselves, that we might continue, with renewed determination, to serve and advocate on behalf of all children and see that no child is left behind.

O God, hear our prayer.

Marian Wright Edelman is president and founder of the Children's Defense Fund and its Action Council, whose Leave No Child Behind® mission is to ensure every child a Healthy Start, a Head Start, a Fair Start, a Safe Start, and a Moral Start in life and a successful

passage to adulthood with the help of caring families
and communities (see www.childrensdefense.org).

Notes

1. Carmen DeNavas-Walt, Bernadette Proctor, and Cheryl Hill Lee, U.S. Census Bureau, *Current Population Reports*, P60-231, "Income, Poverty, and Health Insurance Coverage in the United States: 2005" (2006), 52.

2. Children's Sentinel Nutrition Assessment Program (C SNAP), *The Safety Net in Action: Protecting the Health and Nutrition of Young American Children* (Boston: C SNAP, 2004), 1.

3. See, for example, U.S. Department of Education, National Center for Education Statistics (NCES), *Public Elementary/Secondary School Universe Survey*, 1999–2000; Katharine Browning, Terence Thornberry, and Pamela Porter, "Highlights of Findings from the Rochester Youth Development Study," OJJDP Fact Sheet #103, FS 99103 (U.S. Department of Justice, Office of Juvenile Justice and Delinquency Prevention, April 1999); Robert Sampson, Steven Raudenbush, and Felton Earls, "Neighborhoods and Violent Crime: A Multilevel Study of Collective Efficacy," *Science* 277 (August 1997).

4. U.S. Department of Health and Human Services, National Center on Child Abuse and Neglect, *Third National Incidence Study of Child Abuse and Neglect, NIS 3* (September 1996).

5. Arloc Sherman, *Poverty Matters: The Cost of Child Poverty in America* (Washington, D.C.: Children's Defense Fund, 1997).

6. U.S. Department of Health and Human Services, Administration on Children, Youth and Families, *Child Maltreatment 2004* (2006); U.S. Census Bureau, "Current Population Survey," 2005 Annual Social and Economic Supplement, POV34; U.S. Department of Health and Human Services, Centers for Disease Control and Prevention, National Center for Injury Prevention and Control, WISQARS Injury Mortality Reports. All calculations by Children's Defense Fund.

7. Adapted with permission from Marian Wright Edelman, *Guide My Feet: Prayers and Meditations on Loving and Working for Children* (Boston: Beacon Hill, 1995), 183–84.

ACKNOWLEDGMENTS

Appreciation is due first to the many courageous children and their parents living in poverty. The faces and stories of those we have been privileged to know have inspired us throughout this project.

A debt of gratitude is owed also to the churches and ministries faithfully serving children, who lead the way for other Christians seeking to make a difference. A few are profiled in this book, but there are saints all around us.

Thanks to Randy Frame, the former Judson acquiring editor who launched this project, and to his successor, Rebecca Irwin-Diehl, who graciously shepherded it through many changes. This book has also been enhanced by the guidance and encouragement of National Ministries' staff and others affiliated with the American Baptist Churches' Children in Poverty initiative.

I (Heidi) am grateful to Faith Mennonite Church for their prayers and support for our family. Thanks also to our babysitters who cared for our children so their mother could focus on calling attention to the needs of other children. And thanks to my extended family for providing all that really matters in life. Finally, I express loving gratitude for our children: Maurice, Jacob, and Elizabeth, and the other youth who have found their way into my heart—and for my husband, Jim, who brings joy as parent and partner. Your lives are a gift from God.

PREFACE

Hope for children in poverty begins, as Shannon Daley-Harris puts it, with "a poor homeless baby born to a teenage mother" (p. 159). Jesus experienced childhood from the perspective of a low-income family (see Leviticus 12:8; Luke 2:22-24). Throughout his ministry, Jesus chose to "associate with the lowly" (Romans 12:16), with a compassionate understanding of the struggles and gifts of those without worldly power or prestige. Jesus lifted up the humblest children, those most in need of God's blessing, as a model for those seeking to enter the kingdom of God. After beckoning a child to stand among them, Jesus appealed to his disciples: "Whoever welcomes one such child in my name welcomes me" (Matthew 18:2-5; 19:13-15).

Jesus is still appealing to his followers. Through the pages of this book, the children most in need of blessing stand figuratively in our midst. How will we welcome them in Jesus' name?

In contrast to Jesus' affirmation that the kingdom of God belongs to children (Mark 10:14), "poverty is teaching millions of young Americans that they are not valued, that failure is to be expected, and that hope is futile."[1] In chapter 14 of this reader, James Riley Estep Jr. points out the historic link between poverty and violence to children, both physical and emotional. Children in poverty are doubly vulnerable. They suffer material deprivation, manifest as hunger, illness, dilapidated schools, and unsafe housing. But they also are powerless against the adults and institutions who all too often neglect, demean, and abuse those in their care: parents, often themselves scarred by an impoverished upbringing, who fail to nurture; educational systems that fail to teach; child welfare systems that fail to protect; healthcare systems that fail to provide care; and a government that fails to provide justice.

Thus José E. Velez and Celia Delgado mourn for their inner-city Camden neighborhood: "Children live with a daily expectation of the next bad thing that is going to occur" (p. 5). The hopelessness engendered by poverty begets anger, turned inward in self-destructive behaviors and depression, or outward as violence and delinquency. The damage is unacceptable. The loss of potential is incalculable. By devaluing children's lives, poverty diminishes our society as a whole.

The poverty line is officially defined by inadequate income, the inability to purchase the goods and services necessary to maintain an adequate quality of life. But as Jennifer Coulter Stapleton observes, "Lack of money compounds an intricate web of other social conditions" (p. 18). Persistent poverty entails a lack of cultural and social capital—the web of relationships, connections, opportunities, skills, and cultural know-how that enables children to learn to function productively in society.[2] Those who think of themselves as self-sufficient easily underestimate how much guidance and support from adults they required to become so. Grinding material and social deprivation can beget emotional poverty, or a damaged capacity for self-esteem, self-discipline, empathy, and trust. While most experiences of poverty in this country are short-term, these mutually reinforcing facets of poverty can trap families for generations.

It is tempting to begin our response to poverty with the question, why are children poor? While this is an important inquiry, it tends to become mired in debates framed as personal responsibility versus social justice. The Bible does not allow us to draw easy conclusions about why a family is in need. Parental choices, life circumstances, and economic injustice all contribute to poverty, and often these factors are intertwined. Similarly, we cannot look for simple prescriptions to address poverty: families, communities, government, and religious institutions *all* have a biblical role to play. Assigning blame for poverty leads to heated rhetoric but little action. Like the clever lawyer who sought to evade responsibility for loving his neighbor by questioning, "Who is my neighbor?" (Luke 10:27-29), arguments over causes and prescriptions for poverty too often become a diversion from tending the traveler bleeding in the road.

Rather, guided by the premise that God is calling the church to an active role, Christians need to ask three practical questions. First, what can we do to help relieve the suffering of children in poverty, strengthen their families, and improve the communities in which they live? Children need nutritious food, warm clothes, safe neighborhoods, and loving smiles. As a minister with the LifeShare Foundation, for example, Charles Poole serves families by meeting needs for diapers and utilities, as well as offering spiritual nurture.

Second, how can we help prepare children to lead healthy adult lives in spite of their poverty? The resilience of children is remarkable, but it needs a boost from supportive adults. The "Circle of Courage" curriculum described by Vicki Fogel Mykles is one way of helping homeless children shape a future that does not resemble their past. As Delia Stafford and Vicky Dill assert in chapter 6, helping poor children succeed educationally plays a significant role in expanding their horizons. For the faith community, this entails both assisting struggling students and supporting, or creating alternatives to, struggling schools.

Third, how can we work toward the goal of fewer children growing up in poverty in generations to come? The poverty rate for children in the future "depends not only on how many poor children grow up to be poor adults, but also on how many nonpoor children grow up to be poor adults."[3] We must aim not only to provide opportunities for children to escape the yoke of generational poverty but also to prevent new families from slipping into poverty. From 2000 to 2005, an additional 1.3 million children fell below the poverty level, according to Sharon Parrott and Arloc Sherman (see chapter 9). Children are now among the fastest-growing ranks of the homeless.

We must stop this rising tide. This requires broadening our scope beyond caring for individuals in need to advocating for political, economic, and cultural changes. As Shannon Daley-Harris reminds us, the biblical mandate is "not only to 'love kindness' but to 'do justice'" (p. 98).

This book does not offer a detailed prescription for public policy. Well-meaning people can agree on goals (such as quality education) but disagree on political means of achieving them.[4] But all should concur that decreasing the ranks of poor children will require a shift in our national priorities and a significant investment of funds, both private and public. Despite welfare's shortcomings, we must remember that before the

War on Poverty began in the 1960s, the child poverty rate was 27 percent. If even a flawed government program could cut the poverty rate in half, what might be possible with bolder but wiser public policies that strengthen rather than undermine (or abdicate to) families, communities, and private charities? As Curtis Ramsey-Lucas reminds us, "There is much government cannot do—yet this does not warrant the conclusion that there is little government *can* do" (p. 107). Christians must insist that government do what it can.

And Christians must insist that the church do what it can. Sociologist Susan Mayer concludes that public aid is indispensable to children's well-being, but that "once basic material needs are met, factors other than income become increasingly important to how children fare." Or as a teacher in inner-city Chicago put it, "Money can ease the path, but it doesn't hit deep down where the trouble begins."[5] One of these crucial "factors other than income" that the church can promote is raising children in loving, intact families. Another factor is faith. A growing body of evidence points to religion's influence on positive behaviors and attitudes. In a report on "Religiosity and At-Risk Urban Youth," researchers David Larson and Byron Johnson conclude that church attendance "indirectly reduces delinquency involvement by fostering stronger social bonds, good peer relationships, and high involvement in productive social activities."[6] Churches serve youth as a buffer against the risk factors of an impoverished environment.

Both as citizens and as members of the household of faith, we have an obligation to act on behalf of children in poverty. This book is designed to help readers make an informed response. Section I uncovers the scope and scale of the plight of poor children in America, and the consequences of poverty for children and for our nation. Marian Wright Edelman's "Prayer of Confession" provides a fitting summary of the tragedy of child poverty in our nation. Section II examines child poverty through the lens of specific issues: racial disparities, the child welfare system, welfare reform, working poor families, education, health care, and government programs.

The second half of the book emphasizes that poverty is not the last word in children's lives. Section III offers a theological perspective on children and the role of the church in addressing poverty, with the theme that Jesus has entrusted us with bringing good news in word and deed to the poor and with blessing children in Christ's name. The biblical charge is clear: We cannot truly love God without caring for the little ones in whom God delights.

Above and beyond the tragic statistics is the hope that comes from faith actively expressing itself in love. Throughout the book, ministry profiles model diverse ways to restore poor children's chances for a better life. Since poor children tend to be embedded in broken families, blighted neighborhoods, and dysfunctional institutions, the profiles describe a multifaceted response. These stories also invite us to see children not just as the victims of their fate but as active partners in shaping themselves—and their world—for the better. This theme is captured by a saying at Cookman United Methodist Church: "Youth ministry is when youth begin to do ministry (p. 124)."

The wondrous thing about poor children is that they are, first and fore-most, *kids*. That's why we wanted to ensure the children had their own voice in this book—in the form of youth poetry and crayon-scrawled drawings. The delightful artwork was contributed by children in UrbanPromise's after-school program, which equips Camden's children and young adults with the skills necessary for academic achievement, life management, spiritual growth, and Christian leadership (www.urban-promiseusa.org). Asked to draw something important about themselves, these children from Camden's inner city depicted performing in dance recitals or basketball games, enjoying a playground with friends, going to church with family—activities that caring adult Christians have helped bring into their lives. Of course, the most hopeful thing about these chil-dren is that, as kids, they are still becoming. As Robert Odom writes, "Although their pasts have been defined by poverty, their years to come need not be" (p. 32). What a priceless opportunity God is giving us, to help define each child's future according to God's design! What would the world look like if children were treated the same way on earth as they are in heaven? Zechariah 8:5 gives us a clue: "The streets of the city shall be full of boys and girls playing in its streets." Imagine the exuberant, untar-nished joy of childhood spilling into our public places, filling the streets with the sounds of play and laughter. Let this hopeful vision guide our response to children in poverty.

Notes

1. Robert Odom, *Suffer the Children: The Impact of Poverty on America's Future* (Minneapolis: Love INC, 2006), 4.

2. For more on the different manifestations of poverty, see Bill Ehlig and Ruby Payne, *What Every Church Member Should Know About Poverty* (Aha! Process, 1999).

3. Jens Ludwig and Susan Mayer, "'Culture' and the Intergenerational Transmission of Poverty: The Prevention Paradox," *The Future of Children* 16, no. 2 (fall 2006): 175.

4. Our recommendation is that readers refer to organizations such as Bread for the World, Children's Defense Fund, and Call to Renewal to help shape their political agenda for lifting children in poverty. See Ronald J. Sider, *Just Generosity*, 2nd ed. (Grand Rapids: Baker, 2007) for an overview of a comprehensive policy framework for a just society (see especially 93–94).

5. Susan E. Mayer, *What Money Can't Buy: Family Income and Children's Life Chances* (Cambridge, MA: Harvard University Press, 1997), 148, 156.

6. David B. Larson and Byron R. Johnson, *Religion: The Forgotten Factor in Cutting Youth Crime and Saving At-Risk Urban Youth*, Jeremiah Project Report 98-2 (New York: The Manhattan Institute, 1998), 20; see a summary of the research in Barbara Elliott, *Street Saints: Renewing America's Cities* (Radnor, PA: Templeton Foundation Press, 2004), 80–82. See also Mark D. Regnerus, "Making the Grade: The Influence of Religion upon the Academic Performance of Youth in Disadvantaged Communities," CRRUCS Report (Philadelphia: Center for Research on Religion and Urban Civil Society, 2002), 3.

INTRODUCTION
Making a Difference for Children in Poverty
Heidi Unruh

The three main sections of this book will sketch a portrait of child poverty: its impact on children's lives and on our nation, its complex and interlocking facets, and the biblical imperative of a Christian response. The specter of poverty haunting one out of six children in our nation is oppressive and overwhelming.

Thank God that is not the whole picture.

Various metaphors have been enlisted to describe the multitudes of organizations and individuals engaged in efforts to shape a better future for children: armies of compassion, points of light, harvest workers. Taking on the mantle of Christ's special love for children, ordinary people go to extraordinary lengths to help those trapped in poverty overcome obstacles to the abundant life of God's design. Their ministries declare that children *matter*. They consider their contributions of time, energy, funds, and talents to be a fair trade for a child's smile.

Throughout this book you will find profiles of a baker's dozen of these ministries, presenting a cross section of proven programs that could be imported or imitated in other communities. There are, thankfully, innumerable programs for children in this country equally as noteworthy as the ones on these pages. Several important areas of ministry with at-risk youth are not represented here, such as foster care and adoption programs, child abuse interventions, family counseling, youth entrepreneurship, rites of passage, gang ministry, work with the juvenile justice system, runaway youth homes, teen pregnancy prevention, the arts, scouting programs, and sports leagues. Wherever there are needs, there are people of God with caring hearts and creative ideas.

In some respects, the programs profiled in the following pages are quite different. The ministries display diversity in scope, scale, goals, funding sources, ethnic and denominational backgrounds, and neighborhood contexts. They tackle various dimensions of the spectrum of children's needs, from prenatal health care to an alternative high school. They may be as informal as a home-based homework club or they may be an extensive national organization like Kids Hope USA. They also take varying approaches to the problem of poverty. Some address needs primarily on an individual level, fostering one-to-one relationships with children, such as the mentoring program founded by St. John Baptist Church. Others represent supportive partnerships with community organizations that serve children, such as Nueva Creación/New Creation Lutheran Church's adoption of the nearby elementary school. Other programs, such as the Children's Defense Fund and the Poor People's Campaign for Economic Human Rights, seek to challenge child poverty on a broader scale by organizing church members and poor families to work toward social policies that uplift children.

Despite these differences in characteristics and methods, the shared goal of changing the painful reality of child poverty is a cord that strings together several key ministry principles. What common themes can we glean from this diverse collection of ministries?

1. While expressing their spirituality differently, the ministries draw on deep wells of faith to sustain and guide their involvement with children. As described by Shannon Daley-Harris, ministry with the poor unites people in the "bond of the Holy Spirit, the Advocate, who [calls] them to live out their faith in a God of the last and the littlest" (p. 97).

2. The ministries go to where the hurt is, but they focus on the potential, not the problems. When looking at at-risk children through Christ's eyes, they see not a ticking social time bomb but the blossoming image of God. Thus with the positive attention of mentors, the daughter of an incarcerated parent becomes a mentor to other children through the Amachi program; a bully reached by Kids Hope USA becomes a peer mediator; and Big and Little Brothers become lifelong friends.

3. While addressing urgent needs, these ministries do more than simply put out fires; they look to the future by building character, instilling values, teaching problem-solving strategies, healing emotional wounds, opening vistas, and nurturing hope. The elements of Colfax Community Network's "Circle of Courage" curriculum—independence, belonging, mastery, generosity—help homeless children not only cope with their crisis but also build a better society.

4. The ministries are holistic, addressing both tangible and intangible needs. They understand that God created each child to be whole in body, mind, and spirit, and that poor children do not live by bread alone—though they do need bread. As a banner at Nueva Creación proclaims, love in action incarnates Christ's mission to "preach good news to the poor."

5. The ministries recognize that children suffer from a poverty of social connections as well as material possessions. In a consumer culture, poor children are "invisible at best, humiliated at worst" (p. 103). They often lack healthy role models and adults who believe in them. Ministries can heal children's damaged self-esteem and sense of isolation by nurturing relationships of mutual caring and trust.

6. These ministries celebrate life—from honoring Three Kings Day in Caritas Alegres's youth ministry, to rejoicing with eighth-grade graduates in DUCK's after-school program, to welcoming each new life born to mothers in BabySteps. In this way they "cling to what is good" (Romans 12:9) in the children's families, community, and culture.

7. They connect groups in the community, drawing on the gifts of multiple individuals and institutions. The Cookman Alternative School, for example, developed out of "a network of care and connections" involving a cluster of churches, the public school system, youth social services, and a local university.

8. They demonstrate that there are no shortcuts to justice and compassion. Every program reported encountering obstacles and learning curves along the path to effective service. Like nonprofits everywhere, most of these ministries struggle with resources that fall short of their vision—but that has not stopped them from using what they have to do what they can.

9. Each of the profiles conveys an ethos of joy. Despite setbacks, heartaches, and sometimes personal sacrifice, their leaders would not choose to do anything else. José E. Velez and Celia Delgado writing about the ministry of Caritas Alegres in a deeply wounded neighborhood, testify: "Great joy and spiritual satisfaction comes from following God's purpose, particularly in service to the smallest and least fortunate among us (p. 8)."

10. Each of the ministries profiled got its start when a group of individuals decided to take action. This sounds obvious. Yet it has significance in a broken world where, "The easiest path is simply to accept what seems to be inevitable, while evil conquers the city (p. 5)." Change begins with people standing together to say, "Enough!"

Too often, Christians have followed the easy path. You are invited to walk in the footsteps of the servants of God who have chosen a different route, following the Suffering Servant who gave his life for children. These ministries do not vanquish evil or hardship from the lives of the children they serve. But they do offer a hopeful foretaste of the Reign of God.

Heidi Unruh directs the Congregations, Community Outreach, and Leadership Development Project.

Mariah, age 6

SECTION I
The Lives of
Children in Poverty

1

"It Feels Like We've Been Buried"

Jonathan Kozol

A 15-year-old-student, Isabel, jumps right in. "It's . . . like being hidden. It is as if you have been put in a garage where, if they don't have room for something but aren't sure if they should throw it out, they put it there where they don't need to think of it again."

I ask if she believes Americans do not "have room" for her or people like her.

"Think of it this way," says a 16-year-old named Maria, who is Isabel's half sister. "If people in New York woke up one day and learned that we were gone, that we had simply died or left for somewhere else, how would they feel?"

"How do you think they'd feel?" I ask.

"I think they'd be relieved. I think it would lift a burden from their minds. . . . People in Manhattan could go on and lead their lives and not feel worried about being robbed and not feel guilty and not need to pay for welfare babies."

"Do you think that's how they really look at people in this neighborhood?"

"I think they look at us as obstacles to moving forward," she replies. . . . "It's like—I don't know how to say this . . . ." She holds a Styrofoam cup in her hands and turns it slowly for a moment. "If you weave enough bad things into the fibers of a person's life—sickness and filth, old mattresses and other junk thrown in the streets and other ugly ruined things, and ruined people, a prison here, sewage there, drug dealers here, the homeless people over there, then give us the very worst schools anyone could think of, hospitals that keep you waiting for ten hours, police that don't show up when

2

someone's dying, take the train that's underneath the street in the good neighborhoods and put it up above where it shuts out the sun, you can guess that life will not be very nice and children will not have much sense of being glad of who they are. Sometimes it feels like we've been buried six feet under their perceptions. This is what I feel they have accomplished."

"Put them over there in a big housing project," says a boy named Benjamin. "Pack them tight. Don't think about them. Keep your hands clean. Maybe they'll kill each other off."

"I have a few statements to make about that," Isabel says. "When we talk about the people who are making these decisions we keep saying 'they' and most of the time we think of 'they' as being white. We don't even know who they might really be, yet we keep saying 'they.' This is because we know we have no power to decide these things. Something's always happening where the last and final vote was not the one we made. So we say 'they did this' and 'they' seems extremely powerful, but we do not know who 'they' are.

"Sometimes it seems that 'they' are the welfare workers or the supervisors, who can be very rude to people, or maybe the nurses at the hospitals, or the doctors, or police, but most of these people do not have much power. So you always want to know who does have power and you ask this question but you can't find out. You see destruction around you but you do not know who the destroyer is."

Some people, I point out, "would say that the 'destroyers' are the people right here in this neighborhood." I run through a list of some of the people who are likely to be named most frequently—drug dealers, or the kids whose parents do not give them proper supervision, or teenagers who cause havoc in the housing projects, absent fathers, women who refuse some kinds of jobs that they may find demeaning. . . .

"The drug dealers don't have any power over the economy," Maria says. "They don't control the hospitals. They don't run the schools and they don't run New York."

"Okay, I have a few points to make," says an extremely shy and dark-skinned girl who tells me she is from Honduras.

She speaks softly at first; the others turn to her, and a group of somewhat restless boys who have been whispering to one another quiet down and pay attention.

"My mother can't speak English, so I go with her to welfare. I always feel like crying when I see the way she's treated. 'Fill this application! Hurry up! Sit down! It's not your turn!' This is not the way that people should be treated. . . . I hear this lady say to another lady, to a social worker, or a supervisor, 'Why are they here if they don't speak the language? Why don't they go back to where they're from?'

"But it isn't only language, because no one talks that way to a rich lady who does not speak English. Go downtown. You'll see what I mean. Sometimes these women come from Italy or Argentina or from Spain. They go in the stores in their beautiful clothes. They're treated like celebrities. It isn't the language. It's skin color and it's being poor. This is something more than disrespect. It's as if they wish that you did not *exist* so they would not have to be bothered."

Journalist Jonathan Kozol spent time with the children of Mott Haven, the poorest district in the South Bronx, with a median household income in 1991 of $7,600. Here he records a conversation with teenagers at a youth center about life in their impoverished community.

Excerpted with permission from Jonathan Kozol, *Amazing Grace: The Lives of Children and the Conscience of a Nation* (New York: Crown Publishers, 1995), 38–41.

Song of Comfort for Children

THE FACE OF CHRIST
To the tune of St. Peter

Sometimes when we are hurt
and sad,
And friends are holding us,
We say a pray'r deep down inside,
And see the face of Christ.

Sometimes when we're confused
and lost,
And friends are helping us,
We say a pray'r deep down inside,
And see the face of Christ.

Sometimes when we feel all
alone,
And friends are by our side,
We say a pray'r deep down inside,
And see the face of Christ.

Children's song reprinted with permission from Anne McKinstry, *Sing a Song* (Lee, Mass.: self-published, 2006).

4

MINISTRY PROFILE
Seeds of Hope: Caritas Alegres (Happy Faces) Ministry
José E. Velez and Celia Delgado

How Caritas Alegres Began

Camden, New Jersey, has twice been declared the poorest and most dangerous city in the United States. This city carries scars of poverty, desolation, and abandonment. Dilapidated, boarded-up buildings are everywhere. The drug dealer on the corner, the prostitute walking the street, and the junkie sitting on the steps are the most visible role models for many of our youth. A growing Hispanic immigrant population is estranged from the rest of society. The schools are strained by collisions between diverse cultures. The fear of violence is pervasive. All too frequently, we bury young people who fall victim to this environment. Children live with a daily expectation of the next bad thing that is going to occur. The deep disillusionment and hopelessness have repercussions in the lives of residents on multiple levels—psychological, physical, and spiritual. The marks that this context leaves on people's faces, especially our children, are painful and sad. There is no trust, no hope, and no peace.

Those who try to take action to change their community are often persecuted and victimized, driving good people away from the city. The easiest path is to accept what seems to be inevitable, while evil conquers the city. Thus residents tend to maintain an attitude of perpetual denial or indifference, each household living for itself.

Yet to view the city of Camden from the perspective of the cross is to regard it with the same sacrificial love that led Christ to weep over

Jerusalem. In the end, his blood was offered for the city, and his sacrifice started a revolution that brought life and salvation to the world. When we look through the eyes of faith and hope, we recognize that God continues to do everyday miracles for our city. We see many angry faces, scared faces, sad faces, hungry faces that eventually, through the work of God, can become happy faces.

Our ministry was born out of looking at the city from the perspective of the cross and believing in what God wants to do. It began as an idea, a challenge, a tug of the Spirit. For many years, the dream lay dormant. In 1998, after a challenging Vacation Bible School, First Spanish Baptist Church of Camden approved a proposal to expand its ministry for children and youth to last throughout the year. This ministry was designed as an evangelistic enterprise that would offer a message of life and hope to youth in the surrounding Hispanic community. It was an ambitious proposition for a small congregation like ours, but the time was right.

A group of women from our congregation joined the pastor in shaping the project. Outreach was a main concern, as immigrant families experience many barriers to participation in community initiatives. We started to pray. In 2000, without funding, transportation, or supplies, we started our program, trusting that God would bless our steps of faith. The church agreed to budget funds for the ministry, and donations came in from family and friends in the community. An average of seventy children now participate from our neighborhood, most of them immigrants from Latino countries, along with a number of African American children. Over six years of ministry, we have seen many youth grow into young adults.

How the Ministry Has Served Our Youth

Presenting Jesus to urban youth is the heart and passion of everything that is done in our ministry. Caritas Alegres meets the second and fourth Wednesday of every month, from 6:00 to 8:30 p.m. When the children arrive at church, they are warmly welcomed and sent to play various sports in the church facilities. Recreational time is followed by a bilingual devotional service. The children learn praise songs, read the

Bible, pray, and bring offerings. The remaining time is given to activities such as music, arts and crafts, cooking, and games. Participants also take regular trips to parks, farms, campgrounds, concerts, and other special events. These settings provide a relaxed atmosphere for sharing the gospel, as well as a break from the negative influences of their neighborhood setting. The field trips also enable immigrant children to feel themselves more a part of this nation their families have chosen to make home.

The ministry celebrates two big banquets each year. The first is Thanksgiving. Following a traditional meal, served by volunteers dressed as Native Americans and Pilgrims, food baskets are given out to families in need. During the Christmas season, we celebrate Three Kings Day, a traditional holiday in Latin cultures held on the sixth of January, honoring the arrival of the three wise men in Bethlehem. Our children eagerly anticipate the entrance of the three kings, dressed in their majestic outfits and bearing gifts, sponsored by local businesses. For some children, these are the only happy moments of the holiday season.

The program concludes with our church's annual Vacation Bible School, with music, Bible classes, games, food, special visitors, and a grand picnic as its finale. One of our goals is to turn this week-long program, which draws more than one hundred participants, into a summer camp. Many of our kids have begged us to extend it, as they have little else to do through the long summer vacation. We continue to dream and to pray, trusting in God's provision and timing.

Planting Seeds of Hope

Caritas Alegres offers children a release from the drugs, criminality, prostitution, violent images, broken homes, dysfunctional families, abuse, and abandonment with which they are constantly surrounded. Many of our children are burdened with negative feelings of hate, anger, revenge, inferiority, and insecurities, which are expressed as aggression and violence. These issues impede healthy development and happy lives. Our congregation has come to understand that in response, our calling is to sow the seeds of a new life, like the apostle Paul (1 Corinthians 3:6).

With the Lord's help we are planting seeds of joy and hope in their young lives, even if we do not get to see the final result. Just to win one battle against destruction and suicide is a miracle that only the power, patience, and unconditional love of God can accomplish.

We have prayed with the youth, given them counseling and advice, helped them with homework, referred them to agencies to address various problems, visited their homes, and walked beside them through family crises. What outcomes have we observed? Some youth have developed new openness toward Jesus and the church. Some have done better in school, and others have changed negative behaviors. The ministry has promoted understanding between diverse cultures and facilitated lasting friendships. Most importantly, children have discovered that there are people who care about their lives—and that there is a God who loves them and offers them hope.

Through this ministry, we want the city of Camden to see the church as a living entity that practices what it preaches by showing mercy to all people. Although our main purpose is to help the youth, we believe that our congregation has received the greatest blessings from this ministry. Great joy and spiritual satisfaction come from following God's purpose, particularly in service to the smallest and least fortunate among us. Our rewards are measured in spiritual and relational currency. The seeds of salvation, hope, and love our church has been called to plant are harvested in the smiles and laughter of children.

Rev. José E. Velez is pastor of First Spanish Baptist Church of Camden, New Jersey. Celia Delgado serves as the church secretary, and as a member of the Board of Directors for Caritas Alegres. She also teaches students with special needs.

2
Basic Facts about Low-income Children*
National Center for Children in Poverty
September 2006

*These facts are excerpted with permission from "Basic Facts about Low-Income Children: Birth to Age 18," a fact sheet updated annually by the National Center for Children in Poverty (www.nccp.org). This information was the most current available in January 2007.

What is the federal poverty level (FPL) in 2006?[1]
- $20,000 for a family of 4.
- $16,600 for a family of 3.
- $13,200 for a family of 2.

Is a poverty-level income enough to support a family?
Research suggests that, on average, families need an income equal to about two times the federal poverty level to meet their most basic needs.[2] Families with incomes below this level are referred to as low income:
- $40,000 for a family of 4.
- $33,200 for a family of 3.
- $26,400 for a family of 2.

These figures approximate the average minimum income families need to make ends meet, but actual expenses vary greatly by locality. A family of 4 in Houston needs annual earnings of about $36,000; the same family needs $40,000 in Chicago, and $49,000 in Hartford.[3]

How many children in the United States live in low-income families?
There are more than 73 million children in the United States.

- 39%—28.4 million—live in low-income families.
- 18%—12.8 million—live in poor families.

Children by family income, 2005

Above low income 61%

Less than 100% FPL 18%

100-200% FPL 21%

Have these numbers changed over time?
After a decade of decline, the proportion of children living in low-income families is rising again, a trend that began in 2000.

What are the family characteristics of low-income children?
Parents' Employment
- 55% of children in low-income families—15.6 million—have at least one parent who works full-time, year-round.
- 26% of children in low-income families—7.3 million—have at least one parent who works part-time or full-time, part-year.
- 19% of children in low-income families—5.5 million—do not have an employed parent.

Parents' Education
- 26% of children in low-income families—7.3 million—live with parents who have less than a high school education.
- 36% of children in low-income families—10.2 million—live with parents who have only a high school diploma.
- 39% of children in low-income families—10.9 million—live with parents who have some college or more.

Family Structure
- 51% of children in low-income families—14.6 million—live with a single parent.

■ 49% of children in low-income families—13.8 million—live with married parents.

Does the percent of children in low-income families vary by children's age?

Young children are disproportionately low income. 42% of children under age 6—more than 10 million—live in low-income families.

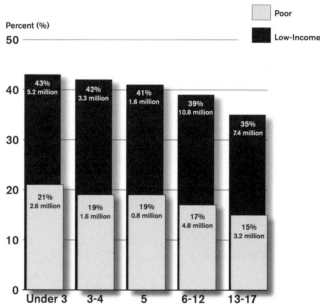

Children living in low-income families, by age group, 2005

Does the percent of children in low-income families vary by race/ethnicity?

■ 61% of Latino children—8.8 million—live in low-income families.
■ 61% of black children—6.5 million—live in low-income families.
■ 28% of Asian children—0.8 million—live in low-income families.
■ 26% of white children—11.1 million—live in low-income families.
Although Latino and black children are disproportionately low income, whites comprise the largest group of low-income children.

Children living in low-income families, by race/ethnicity, 2005

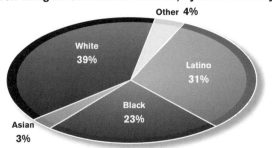

Does the percent of children in low-income families vary by parents' country of origin?[4]

■ 57% of children of immigrant parents—7.0 million—live in low-income families.

■ 36% of children of native-born parents—20.4 million—live in low-income families.

Does the percent of children in low-income families vary by where children live?

Region

■ 42% of children in the South—11.2 million—live in low-income families.

■ 40% of children in the West—7.2 million—live in low-income families.

■ 34% of children in the Northeast—4.3 million—live in low-income families.

■ 35% of children in the Midwest—5.7 million—live in low-income families.

Residential Instability

■ 21% of children in low-income families—5.9 million—moved in the last year.

■ 10% of children in above low-income families—4.4 million—moved last year.

This fact sheet is part of the National Center for Children in Poverty's demographic fact sheet series and is updated annually. Estimates, unless otherwise noted, were prepared by Ayana Douglas-Hall, Michelle Chau, and Heather Koball of NCCP based on the U.S. Current Population

Survey, Annual Social and Economic Supplement, March 2006. Estimates include children living in households with at least one parent and most children living apart from both parents (for example, children being raised by grandparents).

Type of Area

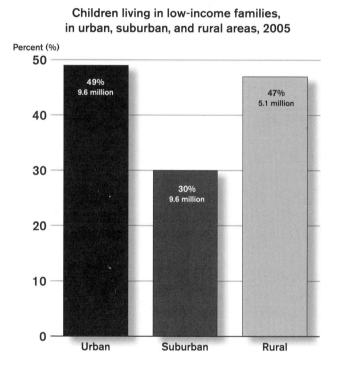

Children living in low-income families, in urban, suburban, and rural areas, 2005

Percent (%)

Urban: 49% 9.6 million
Suburban: 30% 9.6 million
Rural: 47% 5.1 million

Notes

1. These numbers are from the federal poverty guidelines issued annually by the U.S. Department of Health and Human Services. The demographic findings in this fact sheet were calculated using more complex versions of the federal poverty measure—the thresholds issued by the U.S. Census Bureau. For more information on measuring poverty, see NCCP's state profiles and the U.S. Department of Health and Human Services, aspe.hhs.gov/poverty/06poverty.shtml.

2. Berstein, J.; Brocht, C.; & Spade-Aguilar, M. (2000). *How much is enough? Basic family budgets for working families.* Washington, DC: Economic Policy Institute.

3. These figures were derived from NCCP's Family Resource Simulator, www.nccp.org/modeler/moderler.cgi?page=sim_1.

4. Approximately 1 million low-income children ages birth to 18 live in households with one immigrant parent and one native-born parent. Those children are not counted in this figure.

Poetry by Youth Growing Up in Poverty

My Surroundings

It was just like any other day,
The thoughtless air wrapping around each soul
Without a worry, as if pain never existed.

The neighborhood wasn't the best or the worst,
It was just the block where I lived.
My friends, family, and homies added to the despair of life and
   one's choices.
Living happy turned hopeless in an instant.
Instead of feeling the clear blue sky, I felt darkness
Like everything I believed was fading away.

I keep believing that maybe one day our pain of poverty,
Of all the criminal's actions will fade into the wind . . .
But it would be like hoping and praying heaven on earth will arrive.

Tanya (age 16) The poets in these features are youth participants in Neighborhood Ministries (www.neighborhoodministries.org), which cares for the physical, emotional, mental, and spiritual needs of at-risk children and their families in Phoenix. The Neighborhood Ministries Art Center offers kids opportunities in the arts by providing relationships with artist mentors, art-based activity classes, and involvement in Dream Projects. Poems were collected by Art Center director Noel Barto.

MINISTRY PROFILE
"You Don't Remember Me, Do You?":
Fifth Avenue Baptist Child Care Center
Amy White

Ruth Vineyard and Evelyn Greene are used to hearing that question from alumni of the Fifth Avenue Baptist child care program. While Vineyard and Greene can't name all the children they've touched over the years, their work has been recognized as one of the longest running and most successful daycare programs in the Knoxville area by the Department of Human Services and the University of Tennessee.

The childcare center was the dream of Jack Riley, then the church's minister of education. It opened in 1970 with 6 children and 5 employees, including Vineyard and Greene. Within the first year the numbers grew to 120 children and 17 employees. Seeing themselves as missionaries, these workers clearly met a need in their low-income community.

For Vineyard, it was a difficult decision to resign her job and begin full-time, low-paying work at Fifth Avenue. But the rewards have been enormous. Now Vineyard recalls early days when caring for the children was a hands-on experience of mothering: giving baths, cutting hair, shopping for clothes at K-Mart. A church van picked up the children without transportation. During its busiest years the center fed breakfast and lunch to 135 people daily, and offered an after-school program for older children.

Today the center has 49 enrolled children and 10 employees. The family-like feeling of the center is clearly an important component of its success. The need for new workers continues, however. Sandra

Allen, the current director, says the greatest challenge is keeping enough employees.

What sustains the center is its vision as a ministry. "Prayer is key," Allen says. She begins each day praying for the kids, the staff, and herself. God's answers are seen in the lives of the children and in the letters the church regularly receives from appreciative parents. Children who would never end up in a Sunday school class recite memory verses and learn about prayer. Single parents who need help with transportation or financial needs are supported with grace and assistance by the church's volunteers.

Allen explains that at times she feels like a social worker and a psychologist, because "every child must be related to differently." But she has learned that "God is using our young children" and "how important it is for us, as mentors, to be a witness to them." As one thankful parent wrote, "Do you realize what kind of wonderful ministry goes on every single day in your basement?" For more than thirty years, Fifth Avenue Baptist has responded to Jesus' words: "Let the little children come to me . . . for it is to such as these that the kingdom of heaven belongs" (Matthew 19:14).

Reprinted with permission from Amy White, You Don't Remember Me, Do You?" in Salt & Light Guide Book, *Andy Rittenhouse, ed., (Knoxville, TN: Compassion Coalition, 2004), 16.*

3
Poor Children:
The Walking Wounded
Jennifer Coulter Stapleton

Toby and Tina (not their real names) grew up poor. As young children in Virginia, they moved frequently between rented cheap apartments and homeless shelters. Sometimes their mother, Mary, would keep a job for several months and they would stay in one place for awhile. Then she'd lose the job and stop paying the bills, and the electricity or heat would be turned off. Toby would try to do his homework by the light of the street lamp outside their windows. Tina never did much homework. Because she has a severe reading disability, school was frustrating for her.

Meals were scarce in their home. Especially when utilities were off, a cold can of Spaghetti-Os was a typical dinner. Kids at school teased them, calling them "trash diggers" because Mary found some of their clothes in the dumpster behind their apartment building. It was hard to keep the few friends they had, because each move meant starting over at a new school.

Mary had a ninth-grade education and severe mental and physical disabilities. The children didn't have much relationship with their father, who lived in a different state.

When Toby and Tina were in their early teens, the family moved into a long-term housing program for homeless families. There they received the kind of comprehensive care their family needed—counseling for the entire family, tutoring for Tina, life-skills classes, volunteer assistance to help the teens learn how to prepare family dinners. Toby got a part-time job after school and opened his own savings account. For three or four years, the family was stable.

But Mary's health continued to decline, and she died. Now eighteen, Toby has dropped out of school and is living with his friend's family. He is still working part-time and studying for his GED. Tina, sixteen, lives in a residential foster care program for adolescents with emotional problems.

Tina and Toby's story illustrates a stark reality, but not a rare one. In this country, nearly 13 million children—about 18 percent of all children—live below the federal poverty line, which was $16,090 annually for a family of three in 2005. Another 15 million (21 percent of all children) live in homes that are low-income, meaning up to twice the poverty level. Children under eighteen are much more likely to be poor than are adults.[1] A larger percentage of children are poor in the United States than in any other developed country.

African American children are most likely to be poor, with 36 percent living below the poverty line. American Indian/Alaskan Native and Latino children follow closely at 31 and 29 percent respectively.[2] High poverty rates and persistent poverty are disproportionately found in rural areas.[3] Among poor children, 37 percent are extremely poor, with a family income less than 50 percent of the poverty line.[4]

But poverty is more than simply living below a certain income threshold. Children who are poor almost always live in families with a host of other exacerbating issues—parents with low education levels; families led by single young women; violence within the family and the surrounding community; medical problems and disabilities; parental substance abuse; and emotional problems such as depression. So it is hard to isolate the effects of income poverty, but there is no doubt that lack of income makes all of the other problems in poor children's lives more difficult to handle. Lack of money compounds an intricate web of other social conditions.

Whether the problems are caused by poverty itself or by the family and community factors that typically accompany it, many low-income children experience more negative outcomes than their middle- and upper-income peers in four areas: physical, emotional, social, and educational.

Physical Effects of Childhood Poverty

According to a multisite study of more than 20,000 low-income children under three years of age, one in five children do not consistently have enough food for an active and healthy lifestyle.[5] A wealth of health data collected since the 1960s has demonstrated that some of the most striking physical effects of poverty result from hunger and malnutrition.

The following story, reported by a doctor, illustrates childhood hunger in America:

> Maura's mother gets up every morning at 3:00 a.m. and dresses her sleepy four-year-old. Together, they walk through the dark streets to a nearby fast food outlet where mother works the breakfast shift. Maura goes back to sleep under the table in the staff room. On mother's 8 a.m. "lunch break," they get on a bus to take Maura to family daycare, eating forbidden crumbs from the fast food restaurant during the ride. At 12:30, when mother's shift is over, she retrieves Maura and rushes down to the local women and children's shelter for free lunch.
>
> Depending on when mother's paycheck comes, she buys food at the local convenience store and cooks it over the electric hot plate in their one-room apartment for supper. Sometimes instead, she and Maura share a "supersized" cup of French fries and a large soda from the fast food restaurant.[6]

Like the story of Tina and Toby, Maura's story of hunger and poverty is not unique. In fact, it is typical. Households with children are extremely vulnerable to food insecurity, which means sometimes not knowing where they will get their next meal, and to hunger. While nearly 12 percent of all households in the United States experience food insecurity or hunger, the rates are much higher for households with young children (18.5 percent) and for female-headed households, which report the highest rates of food insecurity in the nation (33 percent).[7] For single mothers, ensuring that there is consistently enough food on the table to feed themselves and their children is no easy task.

When children do not get enough healthy food on a regular basis, they suffer more than hunger pangs. A lack of proper nutrition during the critical period between birth and three years can leave lasting physical and mental impairments. Too few or the wrong types of calories during the early stages of life set the course for the rest of the child's life. Growth stunting due to inadequate nutrition is twice as likely to occur in poor children and can lead to decreased mental capacities. The physical and cognitive damage caused by infant and toddler malnutrition is only partly reversible.[8]

Mothers with inadequate nutritional intake during pregnancy are more likely to give birth to a child with a low birth weight. Poor mothers are 80 percent more likely to have a low-birth-weight baby than are middle- and upper-income mothers. Every year, 250,000 low-birth-weight children are born in the United States.[9] Low birth weights increase the likelihood of serious physical disabilities such as blindness, deafness, and cerebral palsy, and can even cause infant mortality. Severe malnutrition in pregnant women has also been linked to an increased risk of schizophrenia when the children reach adulthood.[10]

The problem of hunger in the United States is not a new phenomenon. In the 1930s, pictures of bread lines snaking around city blocks helped to catalyze the federal response to hunger. In the 1960s, a civil rights worker named Marian Wright, who later founded the Children's Defense Fund, led a group of U.S. senators into the Mississippi Delta to show them some of the harshest realities of hunger in America. The 1968 documentary *Hunger in America* shocked viewers with graphic images of starving children—images viewers were more inclined to associate with African and Asian nations than their own country.

More recently, obesity has emerged as a problem of malnutrition far different but just as damaging as a lack of food. Obesity has reached epidemic proportions in the United States, and the problem disproportionately affects poor adolescent girls and women. One study found that 57 percent of women below the poverty level were overweight, compared with only 38 percent of women earning the highest incomes.[11]

The causes are multiple. First, in the United States, foods that are high in starch, fats, and sodium are less expensive than healthy foods like whole grains, fish, and fresh fruits and vegetables. Second, because many low-income families juggle numerous responsibilities and have a poverty of time in addition to a poverty of income, it is faster and easier to eat at a fast-food restaurant or heat up a ready-to-eat frozen dinner than to cook a healthy meal.

Potential problems also arise from how food is consumed among low-income populations, especially by women. When a woman receives her paycheck or food stamps, she overconsumes food because she has been experiencing hunger. But as the month wears on and food becomes scarce in the household, women are typically the first to go without food. A mother will feed men and children and skip meals herself, sometimes going days without significant caloric intake. This feast/famine cycle unbalances her metabolism, causing her body to store large amounts of fat during times of plenty as a way to safeguard against starvation later. These biological changes make the maintenance of a healthy weight more difficult.

The result is that poor women more often suffer serious health problems associated with obesity, including Type 2 diabetes, hypertension, cardiovascular disease, and several forms of cancer.[12] When Mom is unable to work due to health problems and some of the household's limited financial resources must be spent on her health care, the children suffer—as we saw in the case of Tina and Toby.

Lack of safe, affordable housing also has negative health consequences for children. A leading cause of death among poor children is house fires.[13] When families cannot afford to pay for utilities or safe appliances, they are forced to use unsafe alternatives, such as hot plates, space heaters, and candles. The dangers posed by faulty wiring and cheap building materials are often compounded by a lack of functioning fire alarms. Children in low-income housing are also at greater risk of disease due to vermin, mildew, overcrowding, and inadequate heat. The experience of homelessness tends to leave children and their families even more vulnerable to stress-related health problems and physical violence.

Poor families also have limited options when their homes are found to have lead paint. Inhaling the dust from lead paint is particularly damaging to low-income children, because often they are also iron-deficient and anemic due to food insecurity, conditions that make a child more susceptible to the effects of poisoning. One study found that 16.3 percent of poor children have elevated levels of lead in their blood, which causes growth stunting, hearing loss, metabolism damage, impaired blood production, kidney damage, and lower intellectual capacity.[14]

Poverty and Emotional Development

Poor children are vulnerable to two types of emotional problems: antisocial external behaviors such as aggression, fighting, and acting out, and internal difficulties such as anxiety, social withdrawal, and depression.[15]

Sonya Lorelle is the children's therapist at ForKids, the program for homeless families in Norfolk, Virginia, where Toby and Tina experienced a measure of stability. She counsels the formerly homeless children in ForKids' residential and after-care programs, using play and music therapy techniques in addition to traditional methods.

Lorelle describes the biggest barrier facing many of the children she encounters as attachment disorder. She explains that all children are born with the need to bond with other human beings through eye contact, smiles, touch, and being cooed at and talked to. Not receiving this kind of attention can permanently affect a child's emotional development. The formerly homeless mothers at ForKids have been in a state of crisis. They are usually overwhelmed by survival issues and have sometimes been abused. So, while they love their children deeply, they often do not have the time, energy, or skills to start babies off with a stable foundation for emotional well-being.

Lorelle describes a cyclical effect: often the moms did not get the necessary attention when they were young children and so never learned how to provide it for their own children. She explains, "There is a pool inside them that was supposed to be filled up, but it is empty." As a result, poor children may feel hopeless and have a negative worldview. Children with secure attachments have high self-esteem, can cope with stress, and generally believe that even when things are bad, they will get better. Children with poor attachments are more likely to be clingy, less empathetic, less resilient, or antisocial. They often act out aggressively because they would rather have negative attention than no attention. If they are punished for their behavior, it only reinforces their belief that the world is bad and they are bad.

The hope for overcoming this cycle is that attachment is a skill that can be learned. At ForKids, parenting classes that address children's development and needs are mandatory. Lorelle comments, "If we could fix what is going on between the mom and the child, their lives would be better whether they are poor or not."

The Social Effects of Poverty: Two Case Studies

Enjoying healthy emotional and intellectual development is difficult when much of an individual's or family's time is spent coping with crises and trying to survive. These problems are exacerbated when people in poverty are isolated in resource-deprived places like urban slums and remote rural areas. Poor neighborhoods often lack political power and public services. A community is also weakened if many of its people face serious problems like substance abuse, domestic violence, and mental illnesses.

Griffin Centers offers after-school programs for children living in public housing in East St. Louis, Illinois, a city with exceptionally high poverty and crime rates. One of the aims of this program, directed since 1986 by Sister Julia Huiskamp, is to teach social skills through recreation programs that focus on cooperation. Sister Julia explains that many low-income people in her community have low self-esteem, so when they feel even slightly disrespected by their neighbors and relatives, they may retaliate with violence. When teens and young adults lack the social skills and flexibility necessary to succeed in the business world, they sometimes resort to panhandling, prostitution, or selling drugs. As children participate in the program, they learn coping skills and their manners improve. "We give it our best," Sister Julia observes. "But the street is such a pull, so powerful."

Francis Ford is the health care coordinator of Sowing Seeds of Hope, sponsored by the Cooperative Baptist Fellowship in Perry County, Alabama. Ford paints a picture of a community without many social opportunities for children, especially the 50 percent who live below the poverty level. Thirty years ago, the county had several grocery stores, pharmacies, restaurants, and a Greyhound bus station. But now the two major factories have shut down and most businesses have left. A few years ago, the only hospital in the county closed. Except for two fast-food restaurants, there are not many places to socialize in the evenings. The environment does not expose children to people or ideas that could broaden their horizons and stimulate their minds.

The lack of after-school activities, gathering places, and cultural venues in many persistently poor counties in rural America leave the majority of children who live there without opportunities for healthy social interaction and development. This means fewer positive role models, less hope for the future, and diminished motivation to strive for a better life.

Poor Children and Education

Poor children are twice as likely to drop out of school, be held back a grade, or be suspended or expelled as are nonpoor children.[16] Poverty in early childhood has the greatest effects on a child's educational attainment. Children living in poverty are more likely to have lower math and reading achievement scores.[17] An increase of $10,000 in mean family income during a child's first five years is associated with almost one full additional year of schooling.[18] Research shows that the educational level of a child's parents and parental support for education have a strong impact on how far the child goes in school, providing another example of how poverty cycles from parent to child.

At ForKids, where Sonya Lorelle works, most children are a grade level or two behind because frequent moves have caused them to change schools and miss important instruction. Excessive absences are particularly a problem for homeless children.

Sister Julia Huiskamp reports that in one high school in her district, only 11 percent of the seniors "made standards" on their achievement tests. Many children drop out before graduation, some as early as the fifth grade, often because education is not a priority for their families.

Even those who do graduate have often received a substandard education, in part because a low tax base does not pay for highly trained teachers, computers, or up-to-date materials.

The Faith-Based Response: Getting Our Prayers Straight

Bread for the World founder Art Simon recalls a story about an encounter with current Bread for the World president David Beckmann. About twenty years ago, Art approached David, then an economist described as a "rising young star" at the World Bank, for his ideas about how to end poverty. What would make a significant difference in the lives of poor people? Despite all his education and experience as an economist, David answered: "We need to get our prayers straight. If we can do that, everything else will fall in line."

The bedrock of the Christian response to children in poverty must be prayer for hungry and poor people and for the wisdom and strength to work for justice. As we petition God to intervene in the world, the effect on those of us who are praying may be equally necessary. Our worldview and our priorities will be transformed if we pray for hungry and poor people every day.

We must also take action by using our influence as citizens. We can urge our elected representatives to champion policies that help address the root causes of poverty. For example, the federal nutrition programs—including WIC, food stamps, and the school breakfast and lunch programs—are the most direct way to combat food insecurity. They are also proven to increase school attendance, improve academic performance, and decrease behavior problems in the classroom. Although these programs do not meet all the nutritional needs of poor children, millions more would suffer from physical and educational problems without them. In 2005 Christians were the leading voices in stopping proposed cuts to the food stamp program by writing letters, making phone calls, and visiting their members of Congress.

Direct service is another important way of helping poor children. Tutoring in a low-income school, mentoring a child, or working in a food bank or a free health clinic are just a few examples of the many ways to make a difference. Churches and denominations can promote opportunities for Christians to give volunteer time and funds to effective initiatives.

Pray, advocate, serve—these three actions done in conjunction will have a powerful impact. Thirteen million children are waiting.

Song of Comfort for Children

WE BECOME HER FRIEND

To the tune of St. Agnes

When someone's sad and
    feels alone,
A smile would comfort her.
And when that smile becomes
    our smile,
Then we become her friend.

When someone's hurt and
    feels alone,
A hug would comfort him.
And when that hug becomes
    our hug,
Then we become his friend.

When someone's scared and
    feels alone,
A song would comfort her.
And when that song becomes
    our song,
Then we become her friend.

Children's song reprinted with permission from Anne McKinstry, *Sing a Song* (Lee, Mass.: self-published, 2006).

Jennifer Coulter Stapleton, a member of the communications department at Bread for the World (www.bread.org), previously worked with homeless families in Virginia.

Notes

1. U.S. Census Bureau, Current Population Reports, Series P 60-231, "Income, Poverty and Health Insurance Coverage in the United States, 2005" (2006); David Wood, "Effect of Child and Family Poverty on Child Health in the United States," *Pediatrics* 112, no. 3 (September 2003), 707.

2. *2006 Kids Count Data Book: State Profiles of Child Well-Being* (The Annie E. Casey Foundation, 2006), 28.

3. Bruce Weber et al., "A Critical Review of Rural Poverty Literature: Is There Truly a Rural Effect?" Institute for Research on Poverty, Discussion Paper 1309-05 (October 2005).

4. "Child Poverty in 21st Century America: Who Are America's Poor Children?" National Center for Children in Poverty, Fact Sheet No. 2 (September 2005).

5. Deborah Frank, "Child Hunger in the United States: A Doctor's View," *Frontline Issues in Nutrition Assistance: Hunger Report 2006* (Bread for the World Institute, 2006), 67.

6. Ibid., 66–67.

7. M. Nord, M. Andrews, and S. Carlson, *Household Security in the United States, 2004* (Washington, DC: United States Department of Agriculture, 2005), 9.

8. Jeanne Brooks-Gunn and Greg J. Duncan, "The Effects of Poverty on Children," *The Future of Children, Children and Poverty* 7, no. 2 (summer/fall 1997), 58, 80.

9. Ibid., 60, 78.

10. Deborah A. Frank, Statement Before the Subcommittee on Education Reform Committee on Education and the Workforce, U.S. House of Representatives, July 16, 2003.

11. Patricia M. Crawford et al., "How Can Californians Be Overweight and Hungry?" *California Agriculture* 58, no. 1 (January–March 2004), 13.

12. Frank, "Child Hunger," 70.

13. Children's Defense Fund, *Wasting America's Future* (Boston: Beacon, 1994).

14. Frank, "Child Hunger," 70.

15. Brooks-Gunn and Duncan, 62.

16. Ibid., 58.

17. Gordon Dahl and Lance Lochner, "The Impact of Family Income on Child Achievement," Institute for Research on Poverty, Discussion Paper 1305-05 (August 2005).

18. Wood, 709.

MINISTRY PROFILE
Downtown Urban Community Kids (DUCK)
Gayle B. Parker

In 1995, a small group of people from Historic First Presbyterian Church in inner-city Phoenix began a study of Scriptures revealing God's heart for the poor. When they read the story of the Good Samaritan (Luke 10:25-37), one of the class members pointed out, "We don't know our neighbors. How can we be a good neighbor if we don't know them?"

Class members began regular field trips to meet our neighbors. We asked how we could be good neighbors to them, and they told us. One of the things we heard again and again was, "Do something for these kids." We heard it from those who lived in the barrios, those who worked with the youth, and from the principals of the schools. Our church leaders began addressing the need and praying about starting an after-school ministry the following school year. However, in October, one of the principals called with an urgent request to begin it right away. Funding for the limited program they had was being cut off, and she did not want to put her kids out on the street.

The church had the right facility and location but not enough funds or personnel. The pastor and one of the elders agreed to see if God would provide. After the elder found a potential director for the ministry, we met with a pastor from a suburban church that had both funds and volunteers to add to ours, and we proposed a "partnership to do something great for God in the city." Within a few weeks, by the grace of God, we began an after-school ministry to at-risk children in grades K–3, which the children later named DUCK (Downtown Urban Community Kids). The goal was to help the kids succeed in school and keep them off the streets in a fun and safe environment where they were loved by the Lord Jesus and by Jesus' followers.

Within a short period of time, we created a nonprofit corporation, a 501(c)(3). There is an up side and a down side to that, in our experience. Nonprofit incorporation has proven to be very helpful from the standpoint of developing a broader base of funds and volunteer help from outside the church. The church has benefited from several large grants that DUCK received: for example, a new roof for the building, funded largely by a state grant for which the church wasn't eligible to apply. In the last four years DUCK has become financially self-sufficient and able to contribute funds to the church to offset expenses.

At the same time, incorporating DUCK as a separate entity from the church has generated difficult tensions at times and less of a feeling of ownership by church members. We have learned that with the creation of a separate organization, intentional efforts are needed to ensure that church support and commitment grows and that the ministry remains a true mission of the church. In particular, the criteria for selection of executive director, board members, and staff are critical for the mission to remain distinctively Christian.

Without the benefit of a long-term plan, we instinctively decided not to abandon the original kids as they advanced in school, so programming for additional grades was added as we went along. We grew up along with our children. We worked with the teachers in the grade school so that we could track each one's homework and progress. We set up an e-mail system with teachers regarding kids who needed specific help or were likely to fudge on what they needed to work on, and it is not unusual for us to go through a child's backpack to find homework, as well. Rewards and celebrations for school improvement are routine. As we have grown in resources, we have purposely maintained a size that allows us to sustain the community we have formed with students and their families.

A typical after-school day consists of a healthy snack; prayer; group time in which life skills, self-esteem, and biblical values are taught; individual and small-group homework help, reading, and individual tutoring; gym and playground recreation time; arts and crafts; and rotating special activities such as karate, sports, dance, choir, or swim lessons. Field trips and guest speakers are an integral component. DUCK kids also participate in weekly dinners and other church-sponsored programs for children and youth. Partnerships with other organizations, including other churches and businesses, provide additional contacts and resources for ministry participants and staff. In particular, collaborations with Young Life and Wyld Life have been an important blessing to our kids. In the summers, the program is expanded so that kids come for four to six hours each day for educational, recreational, and creative activities.

Nina (not her real name) and her sister were original participants. Nina was five. She learned to speak English in the program. An early major achievement was when she was one of the state finalists in an English essay contest. Through the program, she received scholarships to attend a private college preparatory high school, where she has maintained a 3.9 GPA. The program is now a family affair as her younger siblings attend, and her older sister and parents are active in assisting the program.

Rosita was also an original participant. She comes from a family of eleven children and learned English in the program. She took an accelerated track at a charter school and graduated from high school early with her older brother and sister. Her plans for vocational school training were put on hold when her mother had immigration issues. While her mother's legal status is pending, she has become the primary caregiver in her family. The ministry has provided a place of support and stability for all her siblings, as well as employment for her.

Joanna's story is different. She was eleven when she came. She is being raised by her grandmother and uncle in an English-speaking home, and attends a public high school. She has initiative and leadership and wants to go to college but missed taking the SAT and ACT tests. The ministry was able to link her with a professional college counselor, and as this is written, she is on her way to Washington, D.C., to tour colleges and universities.

Four boys graduated from eighth grade this year. That may not sound to some like a bragging right, but keeping boys in school is a particular challenge. Several boys from difficult home situations are in individual tutoring. The executive director, Elaine Davis, told them she would be at graduation to "be sure they made it," which made the boys laugh—but the truth is, that kind of personal care makes all the difference.

Not surprisingly, DUCK has also made an impact on volunteers' lives. One high school junior from an affluent family was in a rough place personally when he came to volunteer for his community service hours. His encounter with DUCK kids was life-changing. After his service hours were completed, he stayed to volunteer until he graduated—and then helped begin a similar program in the city in another state where he went to college.

In our state of Arizona, each year over 1 out of 10 teens will drop out of school; 1,700 youth are arrested for violent crimes (that's 5 per day); 108 children are killed by guns (more than 2 per week); and the average cost per child in the criminal justice system is $80,000 per year. Considering the high price of doing nothing, the connections we maintain will make a difference!

Rev. Gayle B. Parker is former pastor of Historic First Presbyterian Church in Phoenix, Arizona, and founding pastor of DUCK. Currently she is president of Compelling Communication, a ministry of preaching, speaking, and teaching. For more information, contact DUCK, 602-252-8258, duckinfo@duckkids.org, www.duckkids.org.

4
Suffer the Children: The Impact
of Poverty on America's Youth
Robert Odom

A person's early years should be a time of wonder, of imagination, of innocence. And surrounding it all should be a sense of hope and optimism because the future looks warm and welcoming. But this isn't so for children immersed in poverty. They are denied the joys of youth as well as the promises of happy tomorrows. Reality is, for them, both grim and fixed. A better world is beyond their minds' grasp.

Impoverished children in the United States encounter, cope with, and prevail through hardship and pain that most adults could not fathom, let alone endure. Yet their cry largely goes unheard. There are tragic and unforgivable consequences to not hearing their plea. Although their pasts have been defined by poverty, their years to come need not be.

I have had the opportunity to collaborate with the inner-city and rural elementary school principals who shared the following stories.[1] The situations they describe are compelling, disturbing insights into the way millions of American children live every day.

Hunger

It is astounding and shameful that in the United States, in the land of plenty, more than three million children live in households that are experiencing hunger.[2] Many more millions of boys and girls are food insecure, which means that they have limited or uncertain access to enough food for an active, healthy life. What happens to a child's sense of self-worth when his or her stomach and the cupboards are empty?

> "Weekends are difficult for the children because they don't eat then. Many eat only at school. Kids come to school on Mondays with stomachaches and headaches. Long weekends are the worst. A thirteen-year-old child fainted on Monday. We learned later she was hungry and hadn't eaten since school the Friday before."

> "We had a Thanksgiving dinner for our children with donated food and juice. One nine-year-old told me it was the best Thanksgiving he ever had. It was the first time he had eaten from a real plate."

Homelessness

Families with children represent one of the fastest growing segments of the American homeless population, with more than 1.35 million children experiencing homelessness each year.[3] The acute shortage of affordable housing has caused poor parents and children to be constantly in search of shelter. They move among abandoned buildings, or they "push in" with relatives and friends until there are often several families living in one small, dilapidated, unsafe, and unsanitary apartment. And that is the only home life many of our young people know.

> "Our school starts at 8:45 a.m., but we have kids waiting to get in the building at 6:30 a.m. I don't understand the rules in the homeless shelters. They have to be out at 6:30 a.m., but where are they supposed to go when it's below zero degrees?"

> "One family I know is living in the back of an abandoned truck. I found out about it because the child was coming to school with body odor, so I went to do a home visit. There are six people living in the truck, which is parked on an abandoned lot. We let the children shower here at school."

"The housing here looks awful. There is plastic over the windows and holes on the bottoms of floors. People have no utilities and have to burn candles or use flashlights to see."

"Lots of the brick houses look okay on the outside, but inside they are dismal. We have one family that lives in the basement with all the windows boarded up for security, so there is no light at all. They have a space heater and one cot. A clothesline separates the area where the boy sleeps."

Sickness

Poverty impairs the ability of mothers and fathers to give their families essential medical care. More than 8 million children lack health insurance coverage,[4] and impoverished parents are unable to afford doctor visits. As a result, boys and girls are deprived of preventive measures and even necessary medical treatment.

"The emergency room is the only place our children get medicine. There are no routine checkups. Doctors make referrals to the dentist for braces or fillings, but the parents can't afford to follow up. They care only about the most basic needs—shelter and food."

"We found that 66 out of 70 children in special education classes need glasses. They couldn't read because they couldn't see. And they couldn't see because their parents couldn't afford to buy them glasses."

"The children enter our school from the cold crying and shivering, with their fingers frozen. They aren't wearing any socks or underwear. We had an eight-year-old come to school with frostbite. She lost the tips of her fingers."

"Lots of parents aren't able to store food because they don't have a refrigerator. They'll store food in chests with ice or just eat the food out of the pot it was cooked in. The kids get sick from this."

Violence

What happens when boys and girls experience trauma and terror in their earliest and most vulnerable years? For one thing, they grow up with lowered expectations of what life will be. They also look for a sense of safety and security wherever they can find it, even in gangs. This is one way in which violence and revenge become self-perpetuating and leave their marks on present and future generations.

> "Our children had to write essays for a state test. One girl wrote about how she can't sleep because there's so much shooting, and she's afraid to walk out the door. The state Goals Assessment wrote back saying we needed to pull this girl out for immediate help and get her counseling. But this is how all the children are."

> "These kids are hardened by the time they reach elementary school. They are so angry and already know the world is not a kind place. They insult each other as a way of bonding. They are in each other's face, swearing and hitting as a way to toughen each other up to get ready for the future."

> "There was a drive-by shooting by a kid on a bike. A nine-year-old was standing looking at the bleeding body while eating his ice cream cone. It's the norm."

> "Violence impacts school attendance. Parents take their kids out of school when there's shooting, and they can't go outside because of the gunfire. Or they hear the gunfire from the classroom and know they have to go back out there, or that their mothers and siblings are at home where the shooting is happening. Children come to school tired because the shootings keep them up at night."

Abuse and Neglect

Mothers immersed in a life of poverty and violence frequently become depressed and neglectful of their offspring. Parents with limited means face a mountain of problems and no answers. Their families are hungry. Their living spaces are crowded and run-down. Their unpaid bills pile up. As the pressures mount, they may lash out at the nearest and most defenseless persons, their daughters and sons.

> "Even the kindergartners are so angry. Their little eyes are in a daze because there's so much going on. You can see distress in their eyes."
>
> "The children will come in my office saying they need to use the phone; but then they hang around, and I know they want to tell me something. They'll tell me that dad didn't come home, or their family doesn't want them, or bad things are happening (like incest), or mom is in jail, or they don't have any lights at home, or dad beat mom. They'll fake being sick so they can stay home and try to protect their moms. They think if they're there, the beating will stop."
>
> "School ends at 2:30 p.m., but sometimes we wait until 8 p.m. for parents to pick up their kids. The parents will show up hours late for no reason and then start yelling at their kids. We have to turn in the kids to the child welfare agency if no one picks them up, or they get taken to the police station. Then the children feel that they're the ones who have done something bad."
>
> "You can tell some of the girls have already been forced upon sexually. The incest is unreal. We have a twelve-year-old girl who is pregnant, and I asked her who the dad was. It turns out it was her mother's boyfriend, and the sad thing is that the girl told me her mom doesn't believe her."

Hopelessness

Young children are communicating in dramatic and heart-wrenching ways that their lives are difficult and painful. And many times, that it is too much of a struggle to continue.[5] Many of America's impoverished children have developed a bleak, pessimistic, and limiting view of life. Poverty has deprived them of material possessions and opportunity while leaving them virtually devoid of hope for a brighter future.

"We have a third grader, eight years old, who tried to commit suicide twice by jumping from the school's second floor. We have children six and a half years old trying to commit suicide."

"We had a twelve-year-old boy who was not adjusting. He got into things all the time. He was intimidating. I expressed concern and asked him where he wants to be with his life in five years. He looked me right in the eye and without pausing said, 'I don't have to worry about it, because I'll be in jail or dead.'"

"Our children can tell you how to make a drug sale and how to freebase. Their focus is not on education; it's on surviving. People don't realize how bright these kids are. It's just that the academics aren't relevant. They're just trying to survive."

"At least 50 percent of our students are depressed. We can't motivate them. They don't carry themselves with hope. They don't have a view outside of the community or of a future. Their eyes are hollow; they're not inquisitive. They expect to die young. We're raising a generation of children who are truly in big trouble."

Conclusion

What a powerful cry we have failed to heed. In communities across our country, children are hurt and scarred and discouraged because poverty has taken hold of their lives, their hearts, and their dreams. To break free, children must have much more than full stomachs and clean beds. They need to have their spirits lifted, their broken hearts comforted, and their eyes opened to possibilities that they cannot yet conceive.

As Christians, we have something stronger than the grip of despair. We have faith in God and the power of God's love—and we have hope. We can offer a life-changing message and tangible help to those in need, knowing that through Jesus Christ, all things are possible.

Robert Odom is president of Love In the Name of Christ (Love INC), which mobilizes the church to transform lives and communities in the name of Christ. This chapter is adapted from "Suffer the Children: The Impact of Poverty on America's Future," available from Love INC (www.loveinc.org). World Vision (www.worldvision.org) contributed to the development and text of the report.

Notes

1. The school principals who shared their personal experiences are gratefully acknowledged: Charlotte Blackman, Patricia Gilbert-Parker, Betty Green, Georgia Hudson, Elena Sandoval O'Connell, and Mattie Tyson. Susan Odom assisted with the interviews. Please pray for these people and the many like them who work in challenging and difficult circumstances to give hope to children living in poverty.

2. U.S. Department of Agriculture, *Food Security in the United States: Conditions and Trends* (Washington, DC: author, 2006); America's Second Harvest, *Hunger in America 2006.*

3. World Hunger Year, *Domestic Hunger and Poverty Facts* (2006); National Coalition for the Homeless, "Fact Sheet #2: How Many People Experience Homelessness" (June 2006).

4. Forum on Child and Family Statistics, "America's Children: Key National Indicators of Well-Being 2005, Economic Security."

5. According to the Centers for Disease Control and Prevention, National Center for Injury Prevention and Control, in 2003 suicide was the fourth leading cause of death in the United States for children under eighteen (homicide was the second).

In the Homeless Hotel

Maria P.

Homeless we are called without a place to live,
Somewhere you can call a home,
A place where we can give.
  We are not pigs,
  We're human beings with a race and creed.
  We are not animals that just mate and breed.
Once we were strong . . . but now in a way stronger.
Your pity is not needed because we're poor;
Our pride supports us and helps us endure.
  Your pity is not needed,
    but your understanding,
      yes.
  Being homeless is the saddest thing,
  Because some good people are suffering.
The banging on doors,
The screams in the night,
Even shootings on ground floors,
The pushers in flight.
The homeless scum is what they're called . . .
  But what about me?
  Like you, I once had hopes and dreams.
  But they're growing dim
  And I'm only sixteen.

Reprinted with permission from No Place to Be: Voices
of Homeless Children, *edited by Judith Berck (Boston:
Houghton Mifflin, 1992), 15.*

MINISTRY PROFILE
A Place Homeless Children
Can Call Their Own
Vicki Fogel Mykles

Tammy Herbert, support manager for the after-school program at First Presbyterian Church in Aurora, Colorado, was making star-shaped baloney sandwiches when a gaggle of giggling elementary-school children tumbled through the door. After hugs all around and some eyeballing of snacks, the kids were hustled down the hall to wash their hands.

At first glance it could be any after-school program at any neighborhood Presbyterian church, but it is a highly specialized ministry—a program of outreach to low-income, transient families living, for the moment, in dilapidated motels along East Colfax Avenue in metro Denver. The families of these children, unable to make a living, are denizens of the margins of society.

Families in residential motels are as diverse as any other community. The causes of their homelessness are many—disability, substance abuse, underemployment, lack of skills—but they have one thing in common: poverty. All the families of the East Colfax corridor are well below the federal poverty level, and more than half of the homeless are children.

Many parents who do manage to find work have no choice but to leave their children alone in their one-room homes, supervised only by the electronic babysitter, the television. Children are often bounced from school to school, have no stable relationships with peers or adults, have low self-esteem and poor health, are behind their age levels in educational progress, and are subject to violence.

Aurora's Colfax Community Network (CCN), incorporated in 1999, provides information, services, and programs that strengthen and improve home and community life for these children and their families in the motel trap. The nonprofit organization helps get children enrolled in school; provides a safe, supervised after-school program; tutors children who need help with their schoolwork; teaches social skills; and provides health and nutrition services, mentoring and counseling services, and opportunities in recreation, sports, and cultural activities.

Founder and executive director Maggie Tidwell said CCN uses a model of character development, the "Circle of Courage," that teaches children:

- **independence**—to make decisions and accept the consequences;
- **belonging**—the safety and responsibility of being part of a community;
- **mastery**—a sense of control over self and surroundings; and
- **generosity**—the deep joy that comes from giving from the heart.

Through CCN and its corps of volunteers, children and their parents enjoy family nights with dinner and entertainment; access to community resources and services; assistance in locating apartments and furniture; help with food and clothing needs; job-skills classes; and summer camp. CCN also works with the city of Aurora to help its growing legion of homeless people.

Tidwell is pleased with CCN's success in placing low-income families into stable housing environments in the past few years. "Our goal is to create a safe place where children can come to learn and grow, to feel rooted, nurtured, and motivated," she said. "We offer a place where parents are offered the tools they need to provide for their family's physical and emotional well-being. This is a place the Colfax community can call its own."

Indeed, it's a beacon of hope for the families of East Colfax Avenue.

Rev. Vicki Fogel Mykles is a PC (USA) minister and freelance writer who lives in Fort Collins, Colorado. Reprinted with permission from Vicki Fogel Mykles, from "A Ministry of Hope for Aurora's Homeless Children," Presbyterian Church (U.S.A.) News, *May 28, 2003 (http://www.pcusa.org/ga215/news/ga03055.htm). The Circle of Courage curriculum is described in more detail on the Reclaiming Youth Network website (www.reclaiming.com). For more information about CCN, visit www.colfaxcommunitynetwork.org.*

Prayer of Confession

Marian Wright Edelman

O God, forgive our rich nation where small babies
die of cold quite legally.
O God, forgive our rich nation where small children
suffer from hunger quite legally.
O God, forgive our rich nation where toddlers and
school children die from guns sold quite legally.
O God, forgive our rich nation that lets children be
the poorest group of citizens quite legally.
O God, forgive our rich nation that lets the rich
continue to get more at the expense of the poor
quite legally.
O God, forgive our rich nation which thinks security
rests in missiles rather than in mothers, and in
bombs rather than in babies.
O God, forgive our rich nation for not giving you
sufficient thanks by giving to others their daily bread.
O God, help us never to confuse what is quite legal
with what is just and right in your sight.

*Reprinted with permission from Marian Wright
Edelman,* Guide My Feet: Prayers and Meditations on
Loving and Working for Children *(Boston: Beacon
Hill Press, 1995), 88.*

Joshua, age 9

SECTION II
Special Concerns of Children in Poverty

5
Children of Working Parents Growing Up in Poverty
Charon Hribar and Paul Chapman

Who Are the Poor?

When we lift our hearts to God and pray for the poor, who comes to mind? It's not uncommon to imagine the silent woman on the street corner holding out a cup, surrounded by several plastic bags of clothing, or a lonely man slumped in a city doorway.

But in reality, the poor in the United States represent a large and diverse cross section of the population, including nearly 29 million children in low-income households, averaging six years of age. The great majority of these are the children of working parents.[1] The working poor are not the stereotypical street people whose images dominate our social imagination; they are people far closer to us than we are often willing to admit. Indeed, the chances are that our prayers for the poor include some of the people who are in the pews with us as we pray.

For most people, poverty is not a permanent condition. When a wage earner loses a job or contracts a serious illness, bills soon pile up, the eviction notice comes, and the family is reduced to penury. But often a few months later, with a new job and perhaps a move to a cheaper dwelling, the family begins to climb back. Research by Mark Robert Rank shows that by age seventy-five, three-quarters of Americans have lived at least temporarily below 150 percent of the poverty line.[2] This indicates that falling into poverty is an ever-present potential for most Americans.

If so many members of our society have experienced economic hardships, why are the poor typically depicted as being out of the mainstream of American life? The stereotypes that regard poor people as other portray poverty as a shameful consequence of one's own failures. It is widely believed that the misfortune of poverty can be overcome if only one works hard enough. Members of the University of the Poor suggest, "This individualistic focus not only impoverishes people by denying us the resources we need to survive but impoverishes morality itself."[3] The prevalent assumptions about the personal deficiencies of the poor lead many low-income families to internalize the stigma and hide their economic vulnerability—even to fellow church members. The axiom that hard work is the path to prosperity fails to acknowledge the struggle of the working poor.

At any given time, about one in six children in the United States is living in poverty. These children are not poor because their parents don't work. Approximately 20 percent of low-income children live in households with no work. The rest—80 percent—are children of working parents. About two-thirds of these children have a parent who works full-time, year-round.[4] The reality of extensive though often invisible poverty among working families challenges us to recognize the systemic factors that help to create and reinforce poverty.

Work and Wages

Poverty is a relative experience because the cost of living varies from family to family, and from place to place. One study shows that the wage needed to meet the basic needs of a family of four in Cheyenne, Wyoming, $8.00 an hour, is equivalent to $14.00 an hour in Boston. One way to measure family poverty is to compare income with a self-sufficiency standard that has been calculated for most regions of the country.[5] Consider Santa Clara County in California, for example. In 2003, working families had a median income of $84,000, one of the highest in the nation. According to the self-sufficiency standard for Santa Clara County, a family would need $69,220 a year to live at a basic level without private or governmental assistance. Yet a total of 38,177 children, in 21,000 families, were growing up with incomes of less than $20,000.[6]

A child's risk of poverty is complicated by many social factors that include race, the level of parental education, and whether one parent or two are raising the child. Yet studies suggest that even if race and gender discrimination were eliminated, poverty would still stalk American working families. In 1999, raising a family of four above the poverty line required full-time employment at $9.36 an hour, while 31.7 percent of heads of families worked at jobs paying less than $10 an hour. About a third of the workforce, or about 30 million workers, are not paid a living wage. Among single-parent families, more than half work at jobs that could not raise their families above 150 percent of the poverty line.[7]

Finding employment that pays an adequate wage grows increasingly difficult. The economy has been structured to eliminate jobs by replacing people with machines and sending jobs to other countries where unemployment is high and wages are low. According to the Bureau of Labor Statistics, of the top ten employment opportunities in the next eight years, seven or eight are low-wage jobs. To support their families, growing numbers of workers are forced to cobble together several part-time or temporary jobs with no benefits or job security. Sociologist Mark Rank concludes, "The labor market simply does not provide enough decent-paying jobs for all who need them. As a result, millions of families find themselves struggling below or precariously close to the poverty line."[8]

Poverty trickles down, and the workers on the bottom suffer most. Thirty million manufacturing jobs have been eliminated in the United States since 1970. The displaced workers have had to settle for jobs that pay less, often replacing lower-wage workers who likewise have had to seek still less lucrative employment. This downward spiral is evident in the two counties that constitute Long Island, New York. According to *The New York Times*, the average starting wage for local jobs on Long Island in the last half of the 1990s was $41,000, but by 2005 it plunged to $24,000. "McJobs" in fast-food restaurants, once considered a source of spending money for young people, are now often the primary jobs of family wage earners.[9] As incomes of the top 10 percent of American workers have skyrocketed, the incomes of low-wage workers have stagnated and even inched downwards, even as the cost of living rises.

An important supplement for low-income parents is the earned income tax credit (EITC). The EITC provides a benefit for wage earners with eligible children and income under a certain level. Employers who pay low wages are strong supporters of the EITC, because the government is making up some of the difference between what a family needs to live and what the family receives from the employer. While the EITC makes it possible for many families to survive poverty wages, in an indirect way the benefit is a subsidy for low-paying employers.

The Role of Work in the United States

Work is a core value in the United States. Through work we earn our daily bread and determine our place in society. Typically it is our job that provides health insurance and a pension for old age. From the first time that little children are asked, "What do you want to be when you grow up?" the importance of a job becomes part of our self-image. After meeting someone for the first time, a typical conversation starter is, "Where do you work?" By our employment, we are known. The importance of work in American life has roots in Calvinist teaching that hard work provides a sign of God's grace and sets an example for others.

It is presumed by policy makers that by their labor each person will be able to provide adequately for themselves and their dependents. The ideal that work cures poverty is rooted in the national story. Americans are taught that this nation was built by the arduous work of extending the frontier from the Atlantic to the Pacific, the industrious labors of farmers and factory workers, and the sacrificial efforts of miners and construction workers. Still today, any ambitious person can find a place in the company of loyal workers whose sweat makes the country great.

Yet this narrative leaves part of the American story untold. We must expose the hidden truths of the dedicated workers whose labor has built up our prosperous nation without generating prosperity for themselves and their children. What about the 15 million African slaves and their essential, though unpaid, contribution to the establishment of the American economy? What about the waves of immigrants who suffered intolerable working conditions and abusive and exploitive bosses? What about today's migrant workers whose rights are often violated without recourse? What about the millions of hard-working citizens who cannot make ends meet, despite their best efforts as retail workers, security workers, maintenance personnel, and other low-wage positions?

And we must recognize the children of these workers who have shared in the hardships of their parents: Children of African slaves sold off for their master's profit, never to see their families again. Teenage girls in the nineteenth century driven by economic necessity to work twelve hours a day, seven days a week. Children left behind by parents emigrating to America to earn a living. Today's adolescent minimum-wage workers, many supporting their parents and siblings. And latch-key kids who assume responsibility for care of the household while parents are at low-wage jobs.

These children and their families bear testimony to the reality that hard work is not a guarantee for success and that poverty is not necessarily the product of laziness or lack of determination. The working poor continually fight to be acknowledged as productive members of society and to prove to others—and often to themselves—that these deeply rooted stereotypes do not tell the truth about their struggle.

The Cost of Work

Work can be expensive, particularly for parents of young children who require child care. As much as 25 percent of a single parent's income goes to child care.[10] Many parents are forced to choose between leaving children in unaccredited, nonnurturing, and sometimes dangerous care-giving environments and sacrificing other necessities to pay for quality child care. When a child care arrangement falls through or a child is sick, the parent loses work and income, deepening the family's poverty. While some employers offer child care subsidies or on-site child care, these benefits are unavailable to most low-wage workers. The United States is the only industrialized Western country that does not provide a universal child support subsidy, which might help make work more economically rewarding for poor parents.[11]

A less tangible cost of work is time spent with children. Our society sends contradictory messages about working parents. On the one hand, we recognize that children benefit from spending time with their parents. Parental involvement enhances children's confidence, motivation, and learning skills, giving them advantages as they mature into self-sufficiency. Christian family values promote the ideal of a stay-at-home parent (typically a mom) who can send the children off to school in the morning and be there when the children arrive home in the afternoon. On the other hand, current welfare policies force poor parents to work, thus limiting their availability to protect and nurture their children. While affluent parents are praised for staying home and caring for their children, poor parents are praised for going to work. We provide few systems of support for working poor families to strengthen their family units.

Low Wages and Self-Image

The children of low-wage parents are continually confronted with the degrading reality of their poverty. Submerged in the sea of brand marketing that permeates our society, poor children are often mocked by their peers for their inability to participate in consumer culture. Children may be proud that their parents are working, but they are conscious of the low status attached to low-wage work and the economic pressures that weigh on their parents. The psychological stress on people who are working hard and yet are unable to earn an adequate income is incalculable. If despite your best efforts you still cannot get ahead, you may begin to internalize the failure. Incidents of child abuse are sometimes attributable to frustration over the struggle to make ends meet. Children also may internalize the stereotypes about poor people and develop a negative attitude toward their parents and toward themselves.

While many children manage to rise above their family circumstances, many others are scarred by the effects of marginalization and the fear of a futureless life. The hopelessness associated with menial labor and grinding poverty can promote deep anger and despair in youth. Children who grow up seeing that legitimate work does not pay are more likely to turn to underground sources of income, such as selling drugs. When John Schwarz asked the daughter of a poor working family about her intention to finish high school, she responded with a bittersweet smile, "Why get a high school degree? Both my parents are high school grads and look at them."[12] The damage to poor children's self-image can contribute to destructive choices that carry their poverty into the next generation.

Biblical Reflections on Work

"Anyone unwilling to work should not eat." This verse (2 Thessalonians 3:10) is often cited in support of the American work ethic. But what happens when poor people are willing, but there is not enough work? Or when people work but do not earn enough to eat?

The goodness of work is part of the created order. In the garden of Eden, God calls on Adam and Eve to share in God's creative, constructive activity (Genesis 1:28). Our daily labors, however humble, contribute to the flowering of God's design. God did not intend people to toil for bare survival, though this becomes a consequence of human sinfulness. God intends every able member of society to work and to enjoy the fruits of that labor (Isaiah 65:21-22). Work that does not sustain a dignified standard of life is a violation of God's creative purpose.

To achieve this standard, the Bible is abundantly clear: employers must treat workers "justly and fairly," despite the imbalance of power in employers' favor (Colossians 4:1; see also Malachi 3:5; Ephesians 6:9; James 2:6). For example, Deuteronomy 24:14-15 instructs, "You shall not withhold the wages of poor and needy laborers, whether other Israelites or aliens who reside in your land in one of your towns. You shall pay them their wages daily before sunset, because they are poor and their livelihood depends on them" (cf. Luke 10:7; James 5:4). The ongoing mistreatment of migrant and immigrant workers gives this mandate present-day relevance.[13] The story of Carlos Ramirez is all too common. Carlos and a friend were picked up one morning on a street corner by a woman from an upscale neighborhood who needed help with landscaping. It was hard work, moving stones for a patio; yet at the end of the day, when she dropped them off, she refused to pay the agreed upon $60, claiming she wasn't satisfied with their work. Not only Carlos but also his two children were cheated that day.

Ultimately, God does not tolerate unjust working conditions. God's words to Moses from the burning bush reveal God's deep concern for oppressed laborers: "I have observed the misery of my people who are in Egypt; I have heard their cry on account of their taskmasters" (Exodus 3:7). God directed Moses to rescue the people from their onerous labors. As the people established a new society in the Promised Land, Mosaic law emphasized the principle of fair compensation for labor.

Later, the prophets warned against making a profit by underpaying workers: "Woe to him who builds his house by unrighteousness, and his upper rooms by injustice; who makes his neighbors work for nothing, and does not give them their wages" (Jeremiah 22:13). The warning went unheeded. The gap between rich and poor grew wider. Small farmers, forced to borrow to survive, were charged extremely high interest rates. When they defaulted, the rich landowners foreclosed, a practice condemned by the prophets: "[The wicked] covet fields, and seize them; . . . they oppress householder and house, people and their inheritance" (Micah 2:2). This passage points out how the exploitation of heads of households creates a legacy of suffering for children, often for generations.

The image of God is implanted in every person on earth, regardless of social position. The more each person can reach his or her full potential, the more brightly shines that image. When a child is denied hope for the future, the image of God is hidden. When labor is meaningless and pays so little that children at home are hungry, the inherent goodness of work is thwarted. God's design is that through constructive work, parents may provide their children with all they need to thrive, so that God may be glorified in each precious and unique creation.

Charon Hribar is a master of divinity student who helps coordinate the Poverty Initiative at Union Theological Seminary. Paul Chapman is a community advisor to the Poverty Initiative (www.povertyinitiative.org), which works in the context of the seminary community to build a movement, led by the poor, to end poverty.

Notes

1. John E. Schwarz and Thomas J. Volgy, *Forgotten Americans: Thirty Million Working Poor in the Land of Opportunity* (New York: Norton, 1992), 4; see also David K. Shipler, *The Working Poor: Invisible in America* (New York: Knopf, 2004).

2. Mark Robert Rank, *One Nation, Underprivileged: Why American Poverty Affects Us All* (New York: Oxford University Press, 2004).

3. Noelle Damico, Cheri Honkala, and Ethel Long Scott, "Morality That Impoverishes and the Impoverishment of Morality: Poor Women Resisting," presented at the American Academy of Religion, November 2005.

4. Rank, 286.

5. Six Strategies for Family Economic Self-Sufficiency, "Setting the Standard for American Working Families," www.sixstrategies.org.

6. Applied Survey Research, "2005 Santa Clara County Children's Report: Key Indicators of Well-Being," www.appliedsurveyresearch.org.

7. Rank, 54–60.

8. Ibid.

9. See Katherine S. Newman, *No Shame in My Game: The Working Poor in the Inner City* (New York: Knopf and the Russell Sage Foundation, 1999).

10. On the struggles of single-parent workers, see Kathryn Edin and Laura Lein, *Making Ends Meet: How Single Mothers Survive Welfare and Low Wage Work* (New York: Russell Sage Foundation, 1997).

11. Currently the United States does provide a child tax subsidy, but it is not refundable (i.e., low-income families do not qualify).

12. Schwarz and Volgy.

13. For the impact of migrant workers' struggles on children, see Robert Coles, *Uprooted Children: The Early Life of Migrant Farm Workers* (New York: Harper Row, 1970).

MINISTRY PROFILE
The Work of a Saint: St. John Baptist Church Mentoring Program
Michael Garringer

In May 1992, members of St. John Baptist Church in Columbia, Maryland, organized a meeting to discuss the challenging conditions faced by community residents, particularly young African American males. A decision was made that evening: Ten active church members with a high interest in helping youth formed the St. John Baptist Church Core Mentoring Group. Just like that, a program was born—but a lot of hard work lay ahead.

Designing the Program

The following steps describe the church's process of creating a thoughtfully designed, context-appropriate program that provided quality mentoring services.

1. *Assessing community needs.* The needs of the community and its youth were readily apparent to the church. But in order to make the program effective, community needs had to be more specifically defined. For example, data from the Howard County Public Schools indicated that African American students, especially boys, were not performing as well as other students.

2. *Securing the endorsement of the church.* The core group that brought the mentoring program into being was representative of the community, could articulate the needs of youth, and convinced the congregation to endorse the program. To help it get started, church staff

agreed to donate some support time, and a modest budget was allocated for the program.

3. *Designing the program.* In planning the structure and services of the program, St. John had to answer several questions: What type of mentoring model is right for our church? What types of activities will mentors, youth, and families be involved in, and what services do we offer them? St. John chose to implement a one-on-one mentoring model, with a program design that addresses a full range of participant needs in the areas of school, career, and family:

■ **Academic enrichment:** After-school tutoring sessions involve a mix of church volunteers, school system employees, and teenage peers who conduct most of the tutoring activities under the supervision of the adults.

■ **Values education:** Bimonthly workshops cover a wide range of topics such as personal responsibility, the value of cooperation, the meaning of faith, and self-esteem.

■ **Career awareness:** Workshops address career-focused topics, such as how to fill out an application, tips on preparing for interviews, and acceptable work behavior. Mentors also introduce mentees to employment opportunities and assist in exploring career options.

■ **Parental involvement:** Monthly sessions and support groups for the guardians of participating youth, conducted by a social worker, allow parents to learn about their child's progress in the program, interact with other families, and tap into additional support systems.

■ **Social, recreational, and cultural activities:** Group activities such as camping, concerts, and picnics promote social interaction and enhance cultural awareness.

■ **Community service:** Mentees, with the help of their mentors, annually choose a community service project. This helps build teamwork skills and social responsibility.

■ **Recognition events:** These events include an annual opening ceremony and an end-of-year celebration for all participants. The program also recognizes three exemplary individuals as Mentee, Mentor, and Parent/Guardian of the Year.

■ **Faith involvement:** "Mentors come from a faith community and regard their involvement as an expression of their faith," says program director Doug Pace. "The program promotes character building but does not promote any denomination." While mentors are encouraged to invite mentees to church, youth are not required to attend church services.

4. *Recruiting and training mentors and mentees.* Targeting African American males to be mentors was necessary to reach out effectively to African American boys. While initially mentors were all members of St. John, in later years participation was opened to nonmembers. All mentors commit to at least one hour per week for at least one academic year. They must also complete a criminal background check and provide references. The program offers mentors extensive pre-match training on youth development, communication skills, guidelines for effective mentoring relationships, and strategies for academic improvement and optional religious study.

Youth participants are recruited from the congregation and from local schools. Mentees are given an orientation to the purpose, services, and rules of the program, as well as the value of having a mentor. Because parental involvement emerged as a key to youths' success in the program, this became a requirement for youth participation.

5. *Forming community partnerships.* Recognizing that success and sustainability would depend on support from the community, the core group launched a community awareness campaign, giving presentations to private and public groups about the needs of local youth and how the St. John Baptist mentoring program wanted to help. Having a public school teacher in the core group was invaluable in setting up relationships with local schools. Strategic partnerships were also established with universities, local businesses, and foundations.

Lessons Learned

What can other mentoring programs learn from the experience of St. John's program? Five key elements of the St. John program are particularly important:

■ **A committed, diverse core group of program leaders and advocates.** This group was responsible for planning the program and garnering church support. Their diversity allowed the program to access a wide range of community support and opened doors to partnerships.

■ **Church support.** Administrative support from church staff and the labors of church volunteers enabled the program to reach more youth and offer a wider variety of services. Strong buy-in from church leadership has given the program stability through funding and staff changes.

■ **Community outreach and networking.** Community involvement has aided the program in maintaining mentor involvement, leveraging resources, and developing partnerships that help in accessing and serving youth. Annual recognition programs honor community contributions.

■ **Building trust with mentees and parents.** Pre-match training for mentors lays the groundwork for positive relationships. Listening and communication skills are particularly important in building trust with youth. The program also values parent participation and trust.

■ **Group activities that supplement the one-on-one matches.** While most of the mentoring was through one-on-one relationships, group activities contributed to positive outcomes for youth by enhancing mentees' social relationship skills and fostering a sense of community.

The St. John Baptist mentoring program story began when concerned members of a congregation came together and reached out to the community. With the hard work of volunteers and the right combination of religious, community, and public support, it evolved into a viable program that serves many children and helps connect church, schools, parents, youth, and the community as a whole. Their story can inspire other groups of concerned individuals meeting in churches around the country, wondering how they, too, can help their community.

Adapted with permission from "The Work of a Saint" in The National Mentoring Center Bulletin *(summer 2003): 7–12. Michael Garringer is resource advisor for the National Mentoring Center, which offers training, consultation, and online services for youth mentoring initiatives (www.nwrel.org/mentoring), garringm@nwrel.org.*

6
Empowering Children through Effective Education
Delia Stafford and Vicky Dill

We Face an Enormous and Crucial Task

The large number of children affected by poverty in the United States feels overwhelming: nearly 13 million children. We are failing these millions of children miserably: 7,000 children in our nation drop out of school every school day, predicting a life of poverty for 2,555,000 additional youth and families each year.[1]

In response to the size and the significance of the need, our nation must resolve: No more will we ignore our children—our nation's most precious resource! No more will we stand by as children lack food, clothes, decent housing, health care, or someone to assist with homework. No more should children go to schools in this country where termites infest walls, windows leak, bathrooms don't work, and the building feels like a jail. No more will children receive an inferior, ineffective education or drop out of school.

Righteous indignation is not, however, what we see in the country today, but rather apathy. Most of the time, Christian believers are content in their faith. They are good people who believe they are on the right track in their lives. They may never see the fruit of their apathy in their lifetime, but their grandchildren and great-grandchildren may see a bleaker picture if we continue to sit back and live with the status quo. Accepting the status quo will bring the United States to its knees. And while starting on our knees is an appropriate beginning, sincere people must make an intense examination of what needs to be done to stop the decline of our country's educational system, and act! The next decade must see a radical transformation of the ways we instruct our youth. Graduating every student with an excellent education is the goal, and effective teachers and principals are the key to achieving it.

The challenges facing children in poverty are varied and daunting. Barriers to a quality education include lack of resources in the family to provide the basic necessities of food, shelter, and health care, let alone such comparative luxuries as electronic connectivity, reading materials, tutoring, and a stable environment to support learning. When poor children hit the front door of the school building, further disadvantages accumulate. Under-resourced schools lack adequate space, computer equipment, and other educational materials. Poor children tend to get the nation's lowest paid, weakest, and newest teachers. Facilities are overcrowded and in shameful disrepair. Further, poor parents do not have the capacity to advocate for their children in the school system in the same way that middle-class parents can. Parents frequently work two or three part-time jobs; they may lack confidence in dealing with bureaucracy and confronting educational authorities. High mobility and language barriers compound these challenges.

There is hope in this seemingly unpromising terrain. We have the potential to help each child graduate and gain access to the fullness of the American dream.

Schools Must Empower Children in Poverty—It Is Their Job

Schools are the only institution in this nation at which attendance is compulsory. For most children in poverty, public school is the only choice because other alternatives are difficult to find or impossible to afford.

While other community-based organizations can support learning, their participation is voluntary. Children are not forced to attend the YMCA, Big Brothers/Big Sisters, or church. Because of this compulsory characteristic of the educational system, educational institutions have a special mission to "first do no harm." When schools isolate or track children in poverty, fail to offer them a quality education, and rob them of options for college preparation, they become barriers to devoloping children's potential access to the American dream. Yet the mandatory character of the educational system also represents great opportunity for children who lack other avenues for social advancement.

The Critical Role of Educators

It is not conscionable for this nation to allow children to find school so irrelevant, difficult, or impersonal that thousands drop out daily. Innovations like the smaller learning communities movement, school-to-work programs, and the early college high school initiative have indeed made a difference in many young lives.[2] Yet such national movements are not the only response available to those whose faith calls them to pursue justice for all. Local initiatives that can be handled one school board, one superintendent, and one Parent-Teachers Association at a time may make an even more dramatic difference in the lives of our poorest citizens.

In order to understand the power of local strategies, one must understand the role of school in the lives of children and youth in poverty. One educational researcher who has continued to bring the plight of poor students to the forefront is Dr. Martin Haberman, distinguished professor of education emeritus at the University of Wisconsin in Milwaukee. In *Star Teachers: The Ideology and Best Practice of Effective Teachers of Diverse Children and Youth in Poverty,* Haberman notes:

> For children in poverty being successful in school is a matter of life and death. For those without a high school diploma, the likelihood of ever having a decent job—one with adequate health insurance and some form of retirement account—is extremely remote. Being a drop-out or a push-out dooms people to dead-end jobs, living in unsafe neighborhoods, and never being able to fully provide adequate health care for themselves and their families. It also means that those who are miseducated never develop the individual

potentialities that would give their lives greater meaning and society the benefit of their participation and productivity.[3]

How can we find teachers and principals who agree that school for children in poverty is a matter of life and death? How can we ensure that the leaders of every school see it as their job to identify staff for whom education is a mission?

We need teachers and principals who think of themselves as airplane pilots. You would not want to get on an airplane with a pilot who says, "I'm very good at flying. I fly this jumbo jet every day. I'm very good at taking off as well. I have that maneuver down pat. Now sometimes, I have trouble landing. I land 90 percent of the airplanes I fly. But, you know, win some, lose some!"

You'd get off that airplane right away! Yet children have no alternative except dropping out. The law requires all children to attend school, whatever the condition of their school building. We schedule them into classrooms, regardless of whether the person standing at the front of the class recognizes the vital nature of his or her job, particularly with students in poverty.

Some teachers and principals do set high standards by insisting that all students master basic skills, do well on tests, and graduate. Certainly this is a beginning. However, if this is all they do, our scandalous drop-out rates will continue to climb. Teachers and principals must see it as their central job to motivate and engage students and to make them lifelong learners, problem solvers, and contributors to society. The vision of educators as enablers of social justice is the cornerstone of each school that truly serves children in poverty. It is the rationale for doing whatever it takes to ensure that each child has full opportunity.

It is not enough to close the achievement gap on minimum skills tests so that state departments of education can track improvements on paper. What is needed is a pervasive and shared educational ideology that can make the school the hub of the neighborhood—a place where all youth and their parents are welcomed and served and where the interests of the entire community are promoted. This is the goal of "star" teachers and administrators.

What Beliefs Serve Children and Youth in Poverty?

Star teachers share certain beliefs about their mission to serve children in poverty. The word "beliefs" here refers to people's core values and attitudes on which they base behaviors. In Haberman's observations and interviews with successful teachers, the same practices and principles repeatedly arose. Star teachers and administrators gather their beliefs from a variety of sources—upbringing, faith, philosophy, and life experiences. Regardless of the source, these unshakeable convictions predict who will succeed in the classroom with under-resourced youth.

Teach with persistence. The first core belief is that teachers must be endlessly persistent.[4] Star teachers will not say, "Some get it; some just don't." They will search repeatedly, using every tool in a very large toolkit, to find a way to help each child learn. The belief that it is the job of teachers to keep trying until they are successful helps make their teaching effective. Persistence fosters fruitful teaching by promoting "high expectations for students, the development of teaching skills, teachers' reflectiveness, responsiveness to diversity, teaching efficacy, effective responses to setbacks, and successful use of reformed teaching methods."[5]

When teachers do not believe persistence is the heart and soul of their job, they blame the students for lack of attention, motivation, or capability. What is, in essence, the teacher's lack of persistence becomes a failure on the students' report cards. Acceptance of high failure and dropout rates reveals a paradigm of teaching as a sorting machine, not a supporting environment. The only way to ensure the success of every child is to try endlessly until the magic works.

Protect students as the stakeholders. The second crucial belief centers on preserving learning for students at all costs. Star teachers foster relevant and engaging education by discovering what is "hot" for students as well as what is important for their future, and they explore these subjects via meaningful methods. Star teachers' classrooms often look different from those of teachers who employ more traditional methods and create primarily teacher-directed environments, such as by lining students up in rows or confusing quiet with learning. When relevant forms of instruction clash with the bureaucracy, a star will always opt for the real stakeholder in the organization: the student.

Around Thanksgiving, a teacher brought a turkey into her urban children's classroom. None of the children had seen a live turkey before, and the excitement was palpable. The word spread, and soon some other teachers asked if their children could come see it in its little pen. Groups of happy children filed in and out of this star's motivating classroom. But when a few jealous teachers started raising safety concerns, the principal (clearly not a star) told the teacher to take the turkey home. Although the star teacher managed to bargain one more day out of the principal, the excitement, relevance, and potential lessons of the real-world object were agitated right out of the classroom. The ability to advocate, gently negotiate, and hang on to whatever works with students is a star ideology; in its absence, school becomes irrelevant and students drop out.[6]

Grow in theory and practice. Successful teachers are lifelong learners of more effective and relevant ways to teach. Continuous educator improvement entails bridging theory (what teachers learn from other experts) and practice (how they will apply this in the classroom). Too often, teachers are reluctant to try something new or different; they will repeat their first year of teaching thirty years in a row. Star teachers, by contrast, use multiple sources of feedback, such as test scores, attendance, student conversations, and peer review, to gauge their success in motivating and helping students achieve. They align their ongoing development to their students' needs and seek appropriate ways to apply new learnings. This continual cycle of theory and practice enables good teachers to keep on growing and changing. In low-income districts, star teachers need extra creativity, determination, and insight to adapt teaching strategies for the challenging realities and minimal resources of their context.

Uphold excellence for at-risk students. Amid many factors that cause students to be at risk for school failure and dropping out (such as chaotic home lives, poor nutrition, limited health care, and neighborhood violence), star teachers understand that school itself can put students at even more risk. This occurs when schools sort students into gifted (typically middle- or upper-class) and special needs (typically lower-class) students; when school staff systemically fail to inspire lower-class students to achieve; and when students in poverty are forced into the most run-down schools with the least experienced teachers.

Star teachers view excellent schooling for children in poverty as a requirement of social justice. Equal and excellent education for all means access to high-status jobs for those from poverty backgrounds. Graduates from high school and college have options beyond menial jobs, military service, or jail. Ironically, says Haberman, "For diverse students in poverty the agreed-upon goal of the larger society is to educate them to be happy, compliant losers rather than antisocial ones."[7] The current dysfunctional system diverts quality teachers, principals, facilities, and other resources from those whom we tacitly already consider to be the hopeless losers.

Maintain a professional orientation. Have you ever known a child—perhaps your child—who came home from school and said, "My teacher doesn't like me"? When a teacher's personal feelings toward the learner are transparent, the relationship between the student and the teacher pre-empts learning. Star teachers' relationships with students are professional. Regardless of whether or not they like the child, they will persist in trying to help that student learn. If I only teach the students who meet with my approval, how can I teach the gangbanger or the drug runner? Will I give up on the teenager who is raising a child? Stars build a trust with learners that is independent of students' behaviors or foibles.

Fight bureaucratic burnout. Particularly in districts where the poorest children live, school bureaucracies can wear teachers down. It's not the work; it's the time-consuming bureaucratic processes and interruptions that cause stars to become exhausted. Bureaucracies rank personnel in terms of salary and prestige from high (working in a central office with a large paycheck, far away from children) to low (working with children, with a small paycheck and miserable benefits).[8] Stars opt to accept these disadvantages and relish being with children despite the challenges. They also recognize that these challenges can lead to burnout, and they network with one another to keep children at the center. The antidote to burnout is working together. Maintaining a supportive network, learning from one another, and achieving milestones with children help star teachers avoid high staff turnover.

Keep trust. Everyone makes mistakes, even stars. The key is whether the mistake is allowed to fester and violate the student's trust. Many people still carry the sting of words spoken by a teacher in their childhood that wounded deeply. When a teacher or principal offends a student and then breaks trust by failing to admit to a mistake, learning goes out the window. Adults who cover up, blame someone else, or manufacture excuses cannot model responsibility and conflict resolution. Star teachers and principals realize that breaking trust kills achievement and that the only way to rebuild relational bridges is to apologize.

In summary, all the beliefs of star teachers are interrelated. These core values, attitudes, and beliefs form a seamless ideological profile. Most principals can easily identify their star teachers because they persistently, professionally, and creatively build trusting relationships with their students that generate outstanding motivation and achievement, resulting in higher levels of graduation and college attendance.

Improving the Schooling of Children in Poverty

Identifying the right people to teach is the front door to creating an equitable educational system, especially for students who lack other opportunities for social advancement. Lasting reform at any level cannot take root unless we find ways to recruit, select, train, and support teachers who can build relationships of trust with students. Being highly qualified in the sense of having a teaching certificate, a doctorate, or decades of experience is no guarantee that a teacher will be a star. The seemingly simple but potent step of interviewing designed to identify potential star teachers can make a vital difference for children at risk. Moreover, follow-up is needed to ensure that teachers implement relevant, rigorous, and engaging instruction.

No national policies need be changed for this action step; no prestigious boards need be convened. School by school, if need be, caring people can advocate selection that takes into account applicants' core beliefs related to teaching. Of course, greater investment of resources is also critical, particularly in relation to improving facilities, reducing class size, and providing access to music and arts programs. But without star teachers at the front of the class, successful instruction is unlikely, regardless of resources. Ultimately, star selection is the first and most important step to meet the educational needs of youth in poverty.

Delia Stafford is president and CEO of The Haberman Educational Foundation (www.habermanfoundation.org). Dr. Vicky Dill is director of the Central Texas Alliance for Leadership Development at the University of Texas at Austin and senior researcher at the Haberman Foundation.

Notes

1. Greg Toppo, "Big-City Schools Struggle with Graduation Rates," *USA Today*, June 20, 2006, www.usatoday.com/news/education/2006-06-20-dropout-rates_x.htm.

2. See the website for the Early College High School Initiative, www.earlycolleges.org.

3. Martin Haberman, *Star Teachers: The Ideology and Best Practice of Effective Teachers of Diverse Children and Youth in Poverty* (Houston: Haberman Educational Foundation, 2005), 98.

4. Ibid., 131.

5. Karl F. Wheatley, "Teacher Persistence: A Crucial Disposition, with Implications for Teacher Education," *Essays in Education* 3 (fall 2002), www.usca.edu/essays.

6. Haberman, 139.

7. Ibid., 164.

8. Ibid., 178.

Poetry by Youth Growing Up in Poverty

To the Ones Who Don't Know

I look up at da sky and
  wonder why
We're livin this crazy life
Wondering why I'm still alive
Got all this hate, guilt deep inside
Not tryin to commit suicide
Cause that will make me less
Than who I am
Why don't you understand
These gangsta wayz
Just getting blazed
So we can't think of this heavy
  pain
I can't explain
Da nightmares I have every day

Sonya (age 15) The poets in these features are youth participants in Neighborhood Ministries (www.neighborhoodministries.org), which cares for the physical, emotional, mental, and spiritual needs of at-risk children and their families in Phoenix. The Neighborhood Ministries Art Center offers kids opportunities in the arts by providing relationships with artist mentors, art-based activity classes, and involvement in Dream Projects. Poems were collected by Art Center director Noel Barto.

Promoting Quality Education for Everyone

Dolores E. Lee McCabe

Students: *You determine your destiny!*
■ Master study skills, test-taking skills, and learning techniques.
■ Take responsibility for your own educational achievement.
■ Become advocates for a quality education at your school.

Parents: *Your support is essential to success!*
■ Supplement your child's education through educational enhancement activities.
■ Visit the school. There is power in presence!
■ Contact elected officials about the education budget, school facilities, school safety, and teacher selection standards.

Church: *"Do justice, show kindness!" (Zechariah 7:9)*
■ Provide after-school programs, tutorial programs, and parent workshops.
■ Adopt a local school—bless the school with supplies for low-income students, staff appreciation, facilities improvements, and so on.
■ Confront inferior education by supporting educational advocacy groups.

Community: *You have power—use it!*
■ Organize a coalition to influence educational leaders and government officials.

- Bring your collective voice to school board and city council meetings.
- Encourage informed voting in every election.

Rev. Dr. Dolores E. Lee McCabe is pastor of Millcreek Baptist Church of Philadelphia, former associate professor at Eastern University, and a volunteer with the Good Schools Pennsylvania initiative (www.goodschoolspa.org).

Poetry by Youth Growing Up in Poverty

My Brother

I had three older brothers and Marty was the youngest.
He was my friend, my hero.
We had special moments, but the pain showed more dear.
I was nine years old the first time he got locked up—he was
  only thirteen.

Sadly, I didn't know what was going on or how many places
  he had been.
Maybe I didn't want to realize or even think of what he had
  gone through.
You can never imagine someone you love being in pain.

It was my brother who was by my side—
My brother who cared, not my brother "the criminal."
All I knew is that I was the little sister that he said he would
  take care of.

Tanya (age 16) The poets in these features are youth participants in Neighborhood Ministries (www.neighborhoodministries.org), which cares for the physical, emotional, mental, and spiritual needs of at-risk children and their families in Phoenix. The Neighborhood Ministries Art Center offers kids opportunities in the arts by providing relationships with artist mentors, art-based activity classes, and involvement in Dream Projects. Poems were collected by Art Center director Noel Barto.

MINISTRY PROFILE
Home as a Base for Ministry with Children: The Homework Club
Russ Knight

Although most folks view their homes as places of retreat and rest, home for our family represents headquarters for ministry to our neighbors. When we moved to South Chicago in 1985, God overwhelmingly answered our prayers for a ministry opportunity.

Most of those living on our block are children. It didn't take us long to figure out that we were located in or near the turf of six different gangs. We noted that kids played on our block until after dark without any adult supervision, and that younger kids were being recruited by older gang members, who were using them in carrying weapons and drugs. Not being busy after school makes young children vulnerable to the gang recruiters. We looked for a way to make some of these young people less available to recruiters.

Shortly after we took possession of our home in this new neighborhood, some children rang our bell asking if our kids could come out and play. My wife, Beth, informed them that our kids first had to do homework, and she invited them to come into the house and do theirs while waiting. We discovered that most of these kids had not been in the habit of doing homework. No one at home insisted or checked. Many parents had dropped out of school early or were not native English speakers, and so they felt unempowered to assist their children in doing homework assignments. Thus began the ministry concept called "Homework Club."

The numbers grew slowly that first year until we had almost twenty-five children coming to our house after school for the express purpose of doing homework. A period of time for study and reading is followed by a snack and then games and activities such as arts and crafts until 5:00 p.m. When the school year ends, we reward the faithful either by hosting a party or by sponsoring a trip to a place in the city none of them have been before.

Often Christians do not develop their ministry potential simply because they do not perceive that they have anything special to offer to those around them. I believe that many of the things that we know and do naturally—such as cooking, carpentry, gardening, and parenting— can be extremely valuable to many of our neighbors. I call these bridges to ministry. At the Homework Club, we supply a caring adult (Beth) who has answers to a lot of questions and who is creative, resourceful, fun, and a disciplinarian when needed—not to mention being the best baker in the neighborhood!

While we assist club members in doing their homework, it often becomes apparent that some struggle with reading or math. This is the time to introduce a tutor or find ways to give more attention to the need. Over the years, our own children have gotten involved in helping the club members with reading or math. This has proven to be an ideal way of instilling a sense of mission within the entire family.

"But how and when do you present the claims of Christ to your neighbors?" some have asked. Our response is simply, "All the time." We are always demonstrating who Christ is through our consistent, caring lifestyle. Then, on more occasions than we can count, some child or adult will ask, "Where do we go after we die?" or "Why do you do this—are you rich?" Questions are usually the window to our verbal witness. We also invite the kids to attend church with us.

Several times during the year, we invite individual club members to have dinner with our family. This represents a special occasion for kids who do not often eat solid, healthy meals. Regular mealtimes are rare in their homes. The whole family does not sit around a table and eat together. When we invite neighbors into our home, we demonstrate another model of family life. These times convince us that we are always teaching youth, whether formally or informally.

Urban kids need a great start, or they will never reach their true potential and we will never benefit from the many great things they might have accomplished. The lack of a great start too often leads to mediocrity, drug dependency, jail time, or premature death. We have observed from the Homework Club that many kids from poor or single-parent homes start school well behind other kids. From their first day at school, not much is expected of these kids. Even when a teacher recognizes a student's potential, that teacher is rarely able to count on parental support. We have discovered that many young mothers don't understand the critical role they have in preparing their young for school. They tend to assume that the schoolteacher is solely responsible for educating the children. This insight led us to the concept of a Young Moms Club to teach young mothers how to be involved in their child's education starting in preschool.

As home missionaries, we are committed to using everything available to reach our neighbors with the gospel of Christ. Nothing is off limits— not our house, car, property, friends, or even our privacy. When kids get hurt in the neighborhood, they run to our home for a bandage. During drive-by shootings, our home has served as a safe house until all is quiet. When several families lost everything to a terrible fire, we helped them find food, clothes, and cash through our own contacts. One of the overwhelming benefits of doing ministry out of our home is the marvelous way in which God continues to provide for our personal needs *and* the resources necessary to share with our neighbors. While not rich by this world's standards, we are extremely blessed as we seek to be a blessing to children and their families.

Adapted with permission from Russ Knight, "The Home as a Ministry Base: The Homework Club and Other Ways to Meet Neighborhood Needs," in John Fuder, ed., A Heart for the City: Effective Ministries to the Urban Community *(Moody Publishers, 1999), 466–78.*

A Prayer for Our Schoolteachers and Students

Marilyn P. Turner

Gracious Lord,

We pray this day for our public schools. We pray that parents, teachers, communities, churches, and leaders will come together to obliterate despair and impart knowledge and godly wisdom to students. We delight in the faith that our prayers and actions are transforming schools into havens of safety and laughter, where the spirit of learning and respect engages every person who enters their doors.

O God, give us no rest when we are tempted to immobility by the enormity of the challenges that face our public schools. For the sake of our children, show us how to recover our hope. Transform our feeble wills, fading hopes, and complacent inaction into activism that reveals your heart and miracle-working power. Use us individually and collectively to overcome evil.

We pray for children who have been wounded or disappointed by schools. We pray that students permit wisdom to guide them in the selection of their friends and relationships. May they pursue knowledge, upright lifestyles, and peace. We pray that children are valued and taught to embrace the richness of their own heritage as well as that of their classmates.

Your Word states that it is not your will that even one of these little ones should perish. Ignite within us the desire to pray for students who have lost all reason for hope, so that your little ones may experience a hope that will never die. We commit to pray diligently for schools, teachers, and students, knowing that our prayers will avail much. Amen.

Rev. Dr. Marilyn P. Turner is associate executive director of program ministries, National Ministries, American Baptist Churches USA. Adapted with permission from The Christian Citizen 2 (2004), 5.

7
Health Care Needs of Poor Children
Bruce Jackson

A quiet crisis is emerging for children in the United States. The quality of poor children's health has been declining since 1990.[1] A family's economic resources and access to health care have been found to be key factors in children's health.[2] While health care research pays more attention to the quality of care given to adults than to children, often a medical condition in an adult can be traced to an undiagnosed or untreated childhood health problem.[3] Proper health care for children is too vital to ignore. Yet one in seven children lack medical coverage.

Why is it that poor children experience more health problems than children in families with higher income? While this question has complicated causative factors, four key issues point to opportunities for better health for impoverished children. These issues include unhealthy environments in impoverished communities, lack of access to quality health care, barriers to compliance, and risks for developmental problems.

Unhealthy Environments in Impoverished Communities
Many impoverished children live in homes and neighborhoods that negatively affect their health. Lead poisoning is one of the primary environmental health hazards, because so often poor neighborhoods have aging housing stock, built prior to 1950, still filled with lead-based paints.[4] Lead poisoning can doom a child to lifelong cognitive, behavioral, and physical problems that challenge the child's ability to learn and grow

into a productive citizen, yet it is entirely preventable by addressing housing issues.

Living in poverty exposes children with greater vulnerability to many other diseases. Asthma, a disease that affects the flow of air in the lungs, represents one of many ailments for which poor children currently carry a greater risk. Asthma has a variety of causes, but those who are living in poverty are often exposed to multiple triggers for asthma and allergies, including molds, tobacco smoke, cockroaches, and dust mites. Asthma is a growing concern particularly in impoverished Latino and African American inner-city communities, since these neighborhoods are typically full of environmental asthma triggers. According to researchers at Rice University, "The relationship between poverty and asthma underscores the critical need not only to help those who are desperately poor, but those who hover close to the poverty line where they may be ineligible for all sorts of needs-based social services."[5]

Lack of Access to Quality Health Care

A second threat to the health of children in poverty is the barrier to health care access. Two primary factors prevent children living in poverty from receiving adequate care: lack of medical insurance and lack of health care providers serving in their neighborhoods.

When I moved into the inner city of Pittsburgh, I had insurance and transportation but was unable to find a primary care doctor in my community. I asked my neighbors who did not have insurance or who could not find a doctor who accepted their insurance what they did when they needed to see a doctor. The responses centered around three options. The first group told me that when they needed to see a doctor they would go to the local hospital's emergency room. This expensive form of primary health care becomes an option of choice for many poor families because emergency rooms, by law, cannot turn people away. In addition to being costly to a community as a whole, this form of medical management provides ineffective primary care because it focuses on the urgent, presenting problem with limited, if any, follow up or preventative care. This leads to a pattern of crisis management and diminished overall health. In contrast, when the poor are followed by a primary care provider, the continuity of care generally leads to better patient outcomes. For example, consistent primary care for children allows for tracking the necessary immunizations.

The second option reported by my low-income neighbors was to go to the local clinic provided by the neighborhood hospital. Although this venue did provide them with medical care, continuity of care remained a problem. The clinic was staffed by a rotation of medical residents who were less experienced in diagnosing and caring for patients and often saw a high volume of patients. For these reasons, they tended to focus on patients' presenting problems, with little or no attention to the preventative health care that is so essential for children.

An example of a problem that is poorly managed through a typical hospital clinic is the growing concern of childhood obesity. When my family lived in Pittsburgh, I drove my children to their inner-city school every day. As my children piled out of the car to begin their school day, I would take note of the neighborhood children crossing the street on their way to school carrying chips and soda pop, purchased from the nearby convenience store that also housed a pharmacy. I would muse to myself, "That store has an interesting business plan: Sell chips, pop, and other unhealthy foods to children while they attend school. Then, as the children grow up and develop numerous medical problems from their unhealthy eating habits, they can return to the pharmacy to purchase the medications they need."

Research on health and nutrition among lower-income families has proved the ironic accuracy of these observations. What children need is consistent care that helps their families promote healthy lifestyle choices in the face of poverty. It is difficult to deal with the multiple physical, psychological, and socioeconomic factors associated with obesity in a setting where care is sporadic and focused on acute care needs. When the volume of patients is high, there is little time to reinforce teaching about eating habits.

The third strategy identified by my low-income neighbors was to forgo seeing a health care professional and turn to self care. When health care providers are unavailable in their community, when they cannot afford the medications, tests, or treatments ordered by providers, or when they receive deficient care because of their poverty, parents may attempt to resolve children's health problems on their own. Not only does this disconnect from professional providers limit care for medical needs, but also parents may pass on a habit of avoidance of professional medical care to their children.

One consequence of the lack of access is that poor children fail to receive preventative care. For example, children living in poverty are less likely to receive recommended vaccines compared with their counterparts in middle- and high-income families. Children who are not vaccinated face the increased possibility of illness, reducing their participation in school, physical activity, and social involvement, which can eventually perpetuate the cycle of poverty. Regular preventative care has the potential to make a significant difference in a child's long-term health and to save the family and the community health care dollars over time. The obstacles to quality health care access must be overcome if we hope to reverse the downward trend in the health care of impoverished children.

Barriers to Compliance

Noncompliance means not carrying through with a health professional's plan for a child's care, such as administering medicines, taking a child to get glasses, or changing a child's diet. Environmental and access barriers faced by many poor families contribute to their difficulty with adherence to recommended medical regimens. Parental noncompliance may be due, in some cases, to irresponsibility; but more often, parents do not follow the guidance of health professionals because they are overwhelmed by the complications of living in poverty. Living in survival mode narrows an individual's focus to what is needed to meet the crisis of the day. Families are left with limited time and energy to deal with health care maintenance and prevention.

Another factor in noncompliance is a lack of trust between patient and provider. If a parent feels disrespected or neglected by a health care professional, this diminishes confidence in the provider and willingness to follow the directions for the child's care. Distrust may be exacerbated by language and cultural barriers.

Another obstacle to compliance is the high cost of medications. Parents with limited resources may give their children less than the recommended dosage of a medication or even eliminate the treatment. This can lead to complications and long-term health problems.

Risks for Developmental Problems

The complex issues discussed above conspire to place children born into poverty at a much higher risk for developmental problems during pregnancy and early childhood, leading to long-range consequences. This disturbing trend often begins with inadequate prenatal care of impoverished mothers, leading to poor prenatal development, lack of early detection of congenital defects, and stress factors. Low-income mothers often wait longer to initiate prenatal care compared with women in middle and upper economic classes. Prenatal care is considered a predictor of the health care a child will receive after birth.[6]

Low birth weight is another predictor of developmental problems, including cognitive problems that affect a child's ability to perform in school. "Women living in poverty are far more likely than more affluent women to have low birth and/or pre-term babies, even when known biological or medical risk factors are taken into account."[7]

Lack of access to health care combined with poor prenatal and infant care limits the early detection and prevention of developmental problems, such as impairment of hearing, vision, or neurological function. This can lead to a downward cycle of long-term problems, placing poor children at a disadvantage physically, intellectually, and socially. As a result, they cannot compete in the classroom or in other social arenas.[8]

Recommendations

Communities that search for and commit themselves to solutions to poverty-related health problems have the potential to break the downward cycle and offer impoverished children a brighter future. Some

meaningful programs are already in place. To achieve better health outcomes for poor children, we need more interventions modeled after
these best practices.

One example of an effective program is the State Children's Health
Insurance Program (SCHIP). This cooperative program between the
U.S. Department of Health and Human Services and state governments
provides health insurance for children whose families earn too much to
receive Medicaid but earn too little to afford health care. SCHIP costs
families little to nothing and covers doctor visits, immunizations, hospi-
talizations, and emergency room visits, removing a major barrier for
parents seeking health care for their children.[9]

Another critical opportunity lies in addressing the unhealthy environments in impoverished communities and advocating for safe
housing for the poor. A good first step is to educate people on the
dangers of lead poisoning. Communities can require landlords to
eradicate or seal lead-based paint. Another important step is to support programs that provide safe, affordable housing through new
construction and remodeling projects. An excellent example is
Habitat for Humanity International (www.habitat.org), which "has
built more than 200,000 houses around the world, providing more
than 1,000,000 people in more than 3,000 communities with safe,
decent, affordable shelter." The mission of Habitat is to "eliminate
poverty housing and homelessness from the world, and to make
decent shelter a matter of conscience and action."[10] Habitat is a
tremendous program, but it requires active involvement from volunteers at the local level.

Concerted efforts to promote funding for community health care centers can make a big difference for impoverished children. At the beginning of his first term, President George W. Bush identified an initiative
to add 1,200 Federally Qualified Health Centers (FQHC)—clinics that
provide health care regardless of one's ability to pay.[11] This was a noble
goal, but the full funding for these health centers was never appropriat-
ed. The shortage of funds has limited the number of centers accepted for
federal support. In some cases this has fostered destructive competition
between health centers, as established FQHCs have discouraged other

health centers from acquiring federal funding, rather than working together to help the poor.

The FQHC initiative is an example of a government program that deserves to be expanded. The National Association of Community Health Centers has tirelessly advocated for increased funding. Individuals can promote poor children's access to quality health care by urging congressional representatives to support this initiative, by establishing health centers in poor communities, and by encouraging cooperation among clinics. Christian Community Health Fellowship provides groups with knowledge about how to start a community health center and free clinic.

Compliance is a complex issue to tackle. One solution that has emerged from some community organizations and churches is the use of lay health promoters, who come alongside poor families to "bridge socio-cultural barriers between community members and the health care system."[12] Lay health promoters provide culturally appropriate health education, connect people with needed services, provide informal counseling and social support, administer first aid and health screening tests, and build individual and community capacity. As insiders in the communities where they work, their strategy is to assist people within their circle of family, friends, and neighbors in navigating the health care system, encouraging and empowering them to comply with recommended care.

One of the chief benefits of a lay health promotion program is its focus on prevention. When people learn about risk factors such as obesity, smoking, or inactivity from someone with whom they identify, they may be more motivated to lead healthier lifestyles. As an example of effective proactive intervention, the Friends of the Family ministry in Pittsburgh trains lay health promoters to visit teenage mothers and teach them basic skills in caring for their children. This ministry has helped to reduce infant medical emergencies and deaths.

Conclusion

This brief survey of the complex issues related to health care for poor children has shown the effects of poverty on children's immediate and long-term health outcomes, as well as their development as successful students and eventually citizens of our communities. The negative influence of poverty on health begins during a child's prenatal development and extends through his or her lifetime. Often the consequences of poor health are passed on to the next generation.

The time has come to turn the tide on progress toward better health of children in poverty, until all children are receiving the prenatal care, well baby check-ups, preventative health measures, and medical treatments that they deserve. By working cooperatively, thinking creatively, emphasizing prevention, and dedicating sufficient resources to the goal, we can give all children the chance to lead healthy and productive lives.

Bruce Jackson is executive director of the Christian Community Health Fellowship (www.cchf.org) and serves on the pastoral staff at Lawndale Community Church in Chicago. He formerly served as a pastor in inner-city Pittsburgh and as executive director of a community health center.

Notes

1. Barbara Wolfe, "Poverty, Children's Health, and Health Care Utilization," *FRBNY Economic Policy Review* (September 1999): 9–21. Retrieved from www.newyorkfed.org/research/epr/99v05n3/9909wolf.pdf.

2. U.S. Department of Health and Human Services, *Child Health USA* (2003). Retrieved from mchb.hrsa.gov/chusa03/pages/intro.htm.

3. Sheilale Atherman and Douglas McCarthy, *Quality of Health Care for Children and Adolescents: A Chartbook* (UNC Program on Health Outcomes, University of North Carolina at Chapel Hill, 2004). Retrieved from www.cmwf.org/usr_doc/leatherman_pedchart-book_700.pdf.

4. Centers for Disease Control and Prevention, *General Lead Information: Questions and Answers* (n.d.). Retrieved from www.cdc.gov/nceh/lead/faq/about.htm.

5. Rice University, *Premature Birth Rates Increases Asthma Risk, Study Finds* (2006). Retrieved from www.explore.rice.edu/explore/NewsBot.asp?MODE=VIEW&ID=8095&SnID=3919460. Also *Asthma: A Concern for Minority Populations* (2000). Retrieved from

www.blackhealthcare.com/BHC/Asthma/Description.asp.

6. U.S. Department of Health and Human Services, *Child Health USA*.

7. Rima Shore, *Kids Count Indicator Brief: Preventing Low Birth Weight* (Annie E. Casey Foundation, 2005). Retrieved from www.aecf.org/kidscount/sld/auxiliary/briefs/lowbirthweightupdated.pdf.

8. Pathways Mapping Initiative, *School Readiness Pathway* (n.d.). Retrieved from www.pathwaystooutcomes.org/index.cfm?fuseaction=Page.viewPage&pageID=394.

9. U.S. Department of Health and Human Services, *State Children's Health Insurance Program* (n.d.). Retrieved from www.cms.hhs.gov/home/schip.asp.

10. Habitat for Humanity International Fact Sheet. Retrieved from www.habitat.org/how/factsheet.aspx.

11. Bureau of Primary Health Care, *Health Center Program* (2006). Retrieved from http://bphc.hrsa.gov/chc.

12. American Public Health Association, *Policy Statement: Recognition and Support for Community Health Workers' Contributions to Meeting Our Nation's Health Care Needs* (2001). Retrieved from www.famhealth.org/apha_statement.htm.

MINISTRY PROFILE
BabySteps
Diane Demarest

Moved to "be the heart and hands of Christ in the world," a group of parishioners of St. Michael's Episcopal Cathedral in Boise, Idaho, launched BabySteps in 2003. The ministry aims to reduce health risks to infants and promote their physical, emotional, and mental development. Our mission is to "welcome pregnant and parenting limited-income women into a community of support and education to strengthen families and achieve positive birth outcomes." Through BabySteps, mothers gain the skills and support to be effective, nurturing parents.

The most essential ingredient in any ministry is the will and the heart of a community to come together and take action. With St. Michael's long history of reaching out to the less fortunate in our community (such as through food baskets and free lunches), BabySteps was a natural ministry for our parish. We began with a small group of women—a teacher, a nurse and nurse educator, a pediatrician, and a priest—and spent about six months discussing and discerning this ministry. The next six months were spent networking in the community to explore collaborations and build support. In the first three years since its launch, about 450 women attended BabySteps with their family members and newborns.

BabySteps' program design encourages and rewards health-care knowledge, decision making, and participation. Twice a week, participants attend classes that provide critical information and a supportive atmosphere for sharing about pregnancy, the newborn period, and later infancy. Classes are led by volunteers with expertise in women's health, nutrition, child development, mental health, early literacy, and other related topics. The church provides child care, freeing mothers to focus on learning. An incentive shop offers families additional support. Women earn points for attending classes, making constructive health care choices, and participating in programs conducted by BabySteps' ministry partners. Following class, participants can redeem their points at the BabySteps shop for maternity clothes, diapers, infant clothing, cribs, car seats, strollers, and other infant furnishings. This component provides tangible affirmation for their learning while relieving in a small way the economic pressures of parenting.

While St. Michael's provides the key leadership and vision for the program, as well as financial support through donations and grant writing, BabySteps' design entails a high degree of collaboration. The program relies on more than thirty partner agencies for referrals of eligible mothers, educational resources, and incentive activities and rewards, as well as volunteers. Currently, more than forty-five individuals volunteer at BabySteps each month. About half are professionals from community partners, including health care providers, government agencies, nonprofits, schools, churches, and civic groups. A half-time paid manager coordinates volunteers, organizes resources, and welcomes new participants. We work to build mutually beneficial community relationships. For example, BabySteps provides local university students with meaningful internship experiences in nursing, health promotion, and counseling.

BabySteps focuses on families in poverty because lower-income women, regardless of age and race, are particularly at risk for inadequate prenatal care and poor birth outcomes. Infancy is a crucial period of development, the foundation of competence for the infant and the parents. Poverty, however, starts to influence children well before they are born. Poor mothers are more likely than more affluent mothers to have had a poor health history, to receive inadequate prenatal care, to experience intense and persistent stress through pregnancy, and to abuse harmful substances during pregnancy. These problems are compounded by the social isolation of many limited-income families. BabySteps improves the life chances of children in poverty by helping mothers build a supportive community, parenting skills, and resilience to mediate the stress of poverty. This approach has succeeded in improving birth outcomes among participants. Although 10.2 percent of babies born to low-income women in Ada County are low birth weight, only 1.3 percent of mothers in this program had a baby with a low birth weight.

One unique aspect of this ministry is that it brings women together across economic, educational, and ethnic boundaries. Regardless of our class or culture, we all want the best for our children. Our participants include refugee women from Liberia and Somalia, Hispanic women, teenagers without family support, battered women living in a shelter, former prisoners, and women struggling to get a GED or return to college. The program serves women from many faiths and those with no faith affiliation. The universal connection is our shared parenting experiences and our dreams for healthy and happy children. Nearly all of our volunteers are mothers who understand sleepless nights, worrying about their child's future, the joy of an infant's smile, and the awesome responsibilities of parenting—as well as the life-giving importance of community.

Participants tell us that forming meaningful relationships with other women is one of the most valuable benefits of BabySteps. One volunteer from St. Michael's observes, "Many of the women in the program are really lonely and feeling isolated when they first come here. But then they meet all of the other women, and they compare notes about their babies and parenting. They start to make meaningful, supportive friendships." This note from a program graduate affirms the impact of personal investment: "I thank you for everything, not for just the incentives (which helped out more than you know) but for the knowledge, the friendships, your time, and for your love of our children."

The mother of a BabySteps participant wrote us about her daughter's experience:

> My daughter is seven months pregnant and went to her first BabySteps class today. The class covered what to expect during labor. This is her first child, and she's really anxious. The people were fantastic. They answered all of her questions and really helped alleviate some of her anxiety. She was very excited because she got to pick out an outfit for the baby just for going to class. This was especially great for my daughter because she

doesn't work and lives with her boyfriend, who has three little boys ages two through four. They have very little money and therefore few resources to buy things for the baby, compounding her depression. . . . The education and support this program provides moms and kids are priceless.

What happens during the prenatal period, infancy, and early childhood has lasting echoes in a child's life. By walking with mothers through this critical period, BabySteps makes a difference for a lifetime.

Diane Demarest is project chair of BabySteps at St. Michael's Episcopal Cathedral. BabySteps was one of five finalists in Idaho for the 2004 National Partners in Transformation Award sponsored by the PEW Charitable Trust (find their story on www.fastennetwork.org). For more information, contact westdiane@aol.com, 208-343-1542.

8

Shattered Bonds: Poverty, Race, and the Child Welfare System

Dorothy Roberts

Poverty and Child Welfare

The child welfare system in the United States is rooted in the philosophy of child saving—rescuing children from the ills of poverty, typically by taking them away from their parents. Public child welfare departments that investigate child maltreatment and place children in out-of-home care handle almost exclusively the problems of poor families. Children raised in poverty are more likely to be reported to child protective services, more likely to have the report substantiated, more likely to be removed from their homes, and more likely to remain in substitute care for long periods of time. Poverty—not the type or severity of maltreatment—is the most important predictor of placement in foster care and the amount of time spent there.[1]

Why is the child welfare system filled with poor children? There are three types of association between poverty and child maltreatment: maltreatment may be indirectly caused by parental poverty, detected because of parental poverty, or defined by parental poverty.

There is a high and well established correlation between poverty and cases of child abuse and neglect. The incidence of child abuse and neglect is more than twenty-six times higher in low-income families.[2] Although child abuse occurs in families across income levels, severe violence toward children is more likely to occur in households with annual incomes below the poverty line. Neglect is also concentrated in poor families. One study conducted in Washington State found that 75 percent of a sample of neglect cases involved families with incomes under $10,000.[3] Children from families who receive welfare are at the greatest risk for involvement with the child welfare system, especially for neglect. Researchers estimate that half of the families referred to child protective services received welfare at the time of the referral.[4]

Does this strong correlation prove that poverty causes child abuse and neglect? Not necessarily. Government authorities are more likely to detect child maltreatment in poor families, who are more closely supervised by social and law enforcement agencies. The heightened monitoring of poor families results in the discovery of a great deal of child maltreatment—especially neglect—that would have gone unnoticed had it occurred in the privacy afforded wealthier families. The disproportionate representation of poor parents in the child welfare caseload in part reflects a higher incidence of reporting of child maltreatment in poor families rather than a higher incidence of maltreatment itself. The vast majority of poor parents do not mistreat their children, and there is no inherent psychological or cultural aspect of poverty that makes people prone to violence or neglect.

Many researchers point to stress to explain the association between poverty and child maltreatment. The extreme stress caused by economic hardship and social isolation makes some parents more aggressive toward their children and less able to focus on their needs. Parents consumed by the effort to meet their children's most basic needs may find it difficult to address other family problems. Overcrowded and dilapidated housing exacerbates family friction and is associated with the increased use of corporal punishment.[5] Inadequate food, clothing, and health care, combined with despair that stems from stifled opportunities, are other contributing factors. "When you're overwhelmed with problems—not enough money, no job, how to feed the kids," explains Joy Byers, communications director of the National Committee to Prevent Child Abuse, "it can get so overwhelming that people sometimes lash out at the ones who are most helpless."[6]

Poor mothers often experience elevated levels of psychological distress and depression. These problems are even more common among welfare-recipient parents, with 48 percent of one sample of welfare recipients reporting poor mental health or poor general health.[7] Low-income parents are especially susceptible to diminished feelings of self-efficacy, self-esteem, and life satisfaction, which can negatively affect the ability to parent. The combination of poverty and parental stress is associated with more punitive parenting and the use of harsher punishment.[8]

Not only is stress a regular product of deprivation, but also poor parents lack the financial resources that more affluent parents have to alleviate stress. Poor parents can't afford to seek counseling, hire a nanny, or take a vacation. Neglectful parents tend to have a more stressful life situation with fewer resources to cope with this stress. Most poor parents take good care of their children despite these tensions, but economic hardship has a significant impact on the most vulnerable families. "The conditions of poverty are abusive," writes Renny Golden, "and some families break under the pressure."[9]

The main reason child protection services deal primarily with poor families, however, is because of the way child maltreatment is defined. The child welfare system is designed to detect and punish neglect on the part of poor parents and to ignore most middle-class and wealthy parents' failings.

Child neglect is often the result of parents' financial inability to provide for their children. Parents may be guilty of neglect because they are unable to afford adequate food, clothing, shelter, or medical care for their children. Parental income is a better predictor of removal from the home than is the severity of the alleged child maltreatment or the parents' psychological makeup. After reviewing numerous studies on the reasons for child removal, Duncan Lindsey concludes, "inadequacy of income, *more than any factor*, constitutes the reason that children are removed."[10]

Inadequate housing is frequently at the center of caseworkers' decisions to place children in foster care. Children are routinely kept in foster care because their parents are unable to find decent affordable housing. The court-appointed administrator of the District of Columbia's foster care system determined that as many as half of the children in foster care could be immediately reunited with their parents if housing problems were resolved.[11]

Poverty creates dangers for children: poor nutrition, serious health problems, hazardous housing, inadequate heat and utilities, neighborhood crime. Children in poor families are exposed to residential fires, rat bites, windows without guardrails, and lead poisoning at higher rates than are other children.[12] Children are often removed from poor parents when parental carelessness increases the likelihood that these hazards will result in harm.

A common ground for neglect is leaving a child unattended for long enough to endanger the child's health or welfare. It is more likely that poor children left with inadequate supervision will experience a calamity because their homes and neighborhoods are more dangerous. Many poor mothers have had their children taken away by the state when they have left them alone in the apartment, at a playground, or in the car so that they could keep their jobs. Poor parents also often cannot afford to pay others to care for their children when they are unable to because they are distraught or high on drugs or alcohol. Affluent substance-abusing parents, by contrast, can hire a nanny to care for their children during their absence. The state never has to get involved.

An Iowa court case involved the child welfare department's decision to remove a six-year-old girl from her mother because of the unsanitary conditions they lived in. The apartment was filthy: rooms were strewn with garbage, the sink was overflowing with dirty dishes, closets were stuffed with a combination of clutter and refuse. A majority of judges on the Iowa Court of Appeals felt that the little girl's removal from the home was justified. But a lone dissenter argued that the child welfare agency should have given the mother assistance with cleaning her house. "A few hours of cleaning service would have cost the state less than the judicial time and court appointed fees spent to litigate the adequacy of this woman's housekeeping skills through the state's appellate courts," he added. "And most importantly, the child would not have suffered the trauma of removal and the insecurities that come in foster care."

State child welfare agencies are often willing to incur great expense and inflict huge disruptions on poor families rather than provide for their material needs. Their response to this criticism is that neglectful mothers like the one in this case have a personality deficit that makes them harmful to their children. But wealthier parents who have the same neglectful disposition can hire others (such as a cleaning service) to mitigate the damage to their children. Wealth insulates children from many of the potentially harmful effects of having irresponsible parents.

While child welfare laws punish poor mothers for neglecting their children, welfare reform has been pushing these same mothers into paid employment without the supports needed to care properly for the children. "The goals of welfare reform, which is focused on adult self-sufficiency," warns Mark Courtney, "compete with the goals of the child welfare system, which focuses on safe, nurturant child rearing."[13] For poor mothers, working can interfere with keeping their children out of danger: "off the streets, off drugs, out of gangs, not pregnant, and in school." Yet, "the regular jobs open to unskilled and semi-skilled women were precisely those jobs that are least compatible with mothering," write Kathryn Edin and Laura Lein.[14] These jobs require mothers to work irregular hours and don't provide paid vacations, sick days, or personal time. This makes it hard for mothers who can't afford child care to spend time with their children or check on children left home alone.

Black Child Poverty

There is a persistent and striking gap in the economic status of blacks and whites that shows up in unemployment, poverty, and income.[15] There are dramatic racial differences in a child's risk of experiencing poverty and of experiencing long-term, extreme poverty. The statistics are dismal. Black families are three times as likely as whites to be poor. Poverty researcher Gregg Duncan calculated than among children who turned eighteen between 1988 and 1990, nearly one-half of all black children were poor for six or more years, while only 8 percent of white children spent so many years in poverty.

Especially alarming is the number of black children raised in extreme poverty, with family incomes less than one-half of the poverty line. These are the children at highest risk of being removed for severe neglect. In 1999, more than 15 percent of black children, versus only 5 percent of white children, lived in these dire circumstances.[16] Moreover, black children are the most likely of any group to live in very poor neighborhoods. Even after controlling for family background characteristics, researchers find that living in a low-income neighborhood can negatively affect early childhood development and put children at greater risk of child physical abuse and neglect.[17]

The alarming rates of black childhood poverty are directly related to the racial disparity in the foster care population. The number of children in foster care more than doubled from 262,000 in 1982 to 568,000 in 1999. The enormous growth in foster care caseloads in the late 1980s was concentrated primarily in cities where there are sizable black communities. In 2002, 42 percent of all children in foster care nationwide were black, even though black children constituted only 17 percent of the nation's youth. Black families are the most likely of any group to be disrupted by child protection authorities. Most of the 118,000 children nationwide whose family ties have been severed and who are waiting to be adopted are black.[18]

More and more black children are being placed with relatives, an arrangement known as kinship care. Kinship care has many advantages for black children. It usually preserves family, community, and cultural ties. But it also has a downside. Black children in kinship care receive fewer services than do children in nonrelative foster care and fewer services than white children in kinship care. Many kinship caregivers come from poor or low-income families, like the grandchildren, nieces, and nephews placed in their homes. They are more likely to be single females and to have less income, more health problems, and more children to take care of than nonrelative foster parents.[19] Because black children are the most likely to be placed with relatives, black children in state custody systematically receive inferior financial support and services.

The child welfare system is designed to detect and address neglect in poor families, and black families are disproportionately poor. But does racial bias affect child welfare decision making, even controlling for economic status? In other words, are black families unequally disrupted by child protection agencies because they are black?

Studies show that the actual incidence of child maltreatment among black families is no greater than the incidence among other groups.[20] If black parents are no more likely than others to mistreat their children, how can we explain the racial disparity in the child welfare system's caseload? The federal government has acknowledged that the disparity between the incidence of maltreatment in black families and their child welfare involvement is troubling. A government report suggests that "different race/ethnicities receive differential attention somewhere during the process of referral, investigation, and service allocation."[21]

Child Welfare and Social Justice

Race is critical to explaining why so many black children are removed from their homes by child welfare authorities and placed in state custody. Race is also critical to explaining the harm that black families suffer as a result. Given the disproportionate impact of state intervention on black families and its role in maintaining blacks' unequal status, race must move to the center of public debate about changing the child welfare system.

How can the child welfare system begin to confront the racial disparity in the population it serves? Tackling racism requires altering relationships of power. Changing the relationship between child welfare agencies and the communities they serve means giving the clients more say in the way the system operates. Another strategy is to make child welfare agencies more accountable to the communities where their clients live.

The racial disparity also suggests that we must do more than increasing the resources and improving the management of the present system. The very structure of child welfare is fundamentally flawed. Instead of targeting the systemic reasons for family hardship to prevent child maltreatment, it lays the blame on individual parents' failings after a crisis has already occurred. Instead of supporting families, it punishes them by taking children from their homes for placement in foster care.

We must work toward creating a child welfare system that takes better care of children and pays greater respect to black families, strengthening the ability of black communities to struggle for a more just society. An overwhelming body of research on the negative effects of poverty on children tells us that generous support of child welfare would drastically reduce cases of child abuse and neglect. A truly adequate social welfare system that includes universal income subsidies, health insurance, and child care would cost billions more. But the price is well worth the ultimate savings we will reap in healthier and more productive communities.

Public assistance to poor families and programs dealing with neglected children are two sides of the same coin. Yet compassion toward poor children has always existed in tension with the impulse to blame their parents. The reason that child welfare's problems seem so intractable, writes Nina Bernstein in her book about reforming foster care, lies in "the unacknowledged contradictions between policies that punish the 'undeserving poor' and pledges to help all needy children."[22] Racism has consistently hindered any resolution of this tension but refuses adequate social support for families and hurts black families the most. Only by coming to terms with child welfare's racial injustice can we turn from the costly path of family destruction.

Adapted with permission from Dorothy Roberts, Shattered Bonds: The Color of Child Welfare *(New York: Basic Civitas Books, 2002). Dr. Dorothy Roberts is professor at Northwestern University School of Law and fellow at Northwestern's Institute for Policy Research.*

Notes

1. Duncan Lindsey, "Adequacy of Income and the Foster Care Placement Decision: Using an Odds Ratio Approach to Examine Client Variables," *Social Work Research and Abstracts* 28 (1992); Robert Goerge, Fred Wulczyn, and Allen Harden, "New Comparative Insights into States and Their Foster Children," *Public Welfare* 54 (1996): 12, 15.

2. A. J. Sedlak and D. D. Broadhurst, *Third National Incidence Study of Child Abuse and Neglect, Final Report* (Washington, DC: U.S. Department of Health and Human Services, 1996).

3. Howard Bath and David Haapala, "Intensive Family Preservation Services with Abused and Neglected Children: An Examination of Group Differences," *Child Abuse and Neglect* 17 (1993): 213.

4. Duncan Lindsey, *The Welfare of Children* (New York: Oxford

University Press, 1994); Christina Paxson and Jane Waldfogel, "Work, Welfare, and Child Maltreatment" (Cambridge, MA: National Bureau of Economic Research, 2000); Kristen Shook, "Assessing the Consequences of Welfare Reform for Child Welfare," *Poverty Research News* 2 (winter 1998): 1.

5. Leroy Pelton, "The Role of Material Factors in Child Abuse and Neglect," in *Protecting Children from Abuse and Neglect,* ed. Gary Melton and Frank Barry (New York: Guilford Press, 1994); Robert Hampton, "Child Abuse in the African American Community," in *Child Welfare: An Africentric Perspective,* eds. Joyce Everett, Sandra Chipungu, and Bogart Leashore (New Brunswick, NJ: Rutgers University Press, 1991), 220, 230; Alan Booth, *Urban Crowding and Its Consequences* (New York: Praeger, 1976).

6. Bill Hewitt, "A Day in the Life," *People,* December 15, 1997, 48, 49.

7. Sheila Zedlewski, "Work Activity and Obstacles to Work Among TANF Recipients," *New Federalism: National Survey of America's Families,* Series B, No. B-2 (Washington, DC: Urban Institute, 1999).

8. Vonnie McLoyd, "The Impact of Economic Hardship on Black Families and Children: Psychological Distress, Parenting, and Socioemotional Development," *Child Development* 61 (1990): 311; R. Conger et al., "Economic Stress, Coercive Family Process, and Developmental Problems of Adolescents," *Child Development* 65 (1994): 541; Jeanne Brooks-Gunn, Greg Duncan, and J. Lawrence Aber, eds., *Neighborhood Poverty* (New York: Russell Sage, 1997).

9. Renny Golden, *Disposable Children: America's Child Welfare System* (Belmont, CA: Wadsworth, 1997), 74.

10. Lindsey, *The Welfare of Children,* 155 (emphasis added); Everett, Chipungu, and Leashore, 184.

11. Martin Guggenheim, "Somebody's Children: Sustaining the Family's Place in Child Welfare Policy" (review of Elizabeth Bartholet's *Nobody's Children: Abuse and Neglect, Foster Drift, and the Adoption Alternative*), *Harvard Law Review* 113 (June 2000), 1724.

12. Leroy Pelton, *For Reasons of Poverty: A Critical Analysis of the Public Child Welfare System in the United States* (Westport, CT: Praeger, 1989), 146.

13. Mark Courtney, "The Costs of Child Protection in the Context of Welfare Reform," *Future of Children* (spring 1988), 101.

14. Kathryn Edin and Laura Lein, *Making Ends Meet: How Single Mothers Survive Welfare and Low-Wage Work* (New York: Russell Sage Foundation, 1997), 7, 8.

15. Michael Dawson, *Behind the Mule: Race and Class in African American Politics* (Princeton, N.J.: Princeton University Press, 1994).

16. Joseph Dalaker and Bernadette Proctor, U.S. Census Bureau, Current Population Reports, Series P60-210, *Poverty in the United States: 1999* (Washington, DC: U.S. Government Printing Office, 2000).

17. Jeanne Brooks-Gunn et al., "Do Neighborhoods Influence Child Adolescent Behavior?" *American Journal of Sociology* 99 (1994): 353; Bill Gillham et al., "Unemployment Rates, Single Parent Density, and Indices of Child Poverty: Their Relationship to Different Categories of Child Abuse and Neglect," *Child Abuse and Neglect* 22 (1998): 79, 88.

18. Administration for Children and Families, U.S. Department of Health and Human Services, "The AFCARS Report: Current Estimates as of October 2000."

19. Madeline Kurtz, "The Purchase of Families into Foster Care: Two Case Studies and the Lessons They Teach," *Connecticut Law Review* 26 (1994); James Gleeson, "Kinship Care as a Child Welfare Service: The Policy Debate in an Era of Welfare Reform," *Child Welfare* 75 (1996); Jill Berrick et al., "A Comparison of Kinship Foster Homes and Foster Family Homes: Implications for Kinship Foster Care as Family Preservation," *Children and Youth Services Review* 16 (1994).

20. Toshio Tatara, "Overview of Child Abuse and Neglect," in *Child Welfare: An Africentric Perspective,* eds. Joyce Everett, Sandra Chipungu, and Bogart Leashore (New Brunswick, NJ: Rutgers University Press, 1991).

21. U.S. Department of Health and Human Services, Children's Bureau, National Study of Protective, Preventative, and Reunification Services Delivered to Children and Their Families (Washington, DC: U.S. Government Printing Office, 1997); Sedlak and Broadhurst.

22. Nina Bernstein, *The Lost Children of Wilder: The Epic Struggle to Change Foster Care* (New York: Pantheon, 2001), xii.

MINISTRY PROFILE
Children's Defense Fund: Promoting Faithful Advocacy for Children
Shannon Daley-Harris

On a crisp October Sunday, as you enter Mount Olivet United Methodist Church in Arlington, Virginia, you notice something is different. A yard sign proclaims "Children's Sabbath," and children greet you at the door to the sanctuary with devotional guides reflecting on Scripture's message in light of unconscionable child poverty. Inside the sanctuary, the walls are adorned with posters created during Sunday school sessions studying the needs of children and the response of faith. Hymns, Scripture readings, litanies, and prayers all lift up the urgent needs of children and God's call to compassion and justice. Slips of paper with prayers for children in poverty flutter from clotheslines strung around the sanctuary. Images of children are projected on the sanctuary walls as the preacher proclaims a passionate call to do justice for poor children.

In the fellowship hall, you discover tables displaying opportunities to participate in improving children's lives for the long haul. You are invited to join a child advocacy committee, or to sign up to build a Habitat for Humanity house for a poor family, or to participate in a parenting education series. There's a counter where you can purchase goods with the proceeds donated to an organization helping abused and neglected children. You can attend a forum on faith and children in poverty to learn more about how you can be a voice for justice.

Today's message isn't a typical children's sermon, characterized by sweetness and innocence. It's about one in six children in our rich nation living in poverty. It's about hunger that stalks 13 million children. It's about one in seven children without health care. And unlike many Youth Sundays in which young people plan the service and adults sit back as an appreciative audience, this service asks what each of us will do to make our nation just for all children.

So what's going on here? Mount Olivet is celebrating the National Observance of Children's Sabbaths, when thousands of congregations lift up the urgent needs of children; explore the biblical mandates to care for the poorest, youngest, and most vulnerable among us; and discern ways we can respond through prayer, hands-on service, and justice-seeking advocacy.

The insight and inspiration from the Children's Sabbath goes beyond the third weekend of each October. The event provides a springboard for congregational initiatives such as housing a child care program, creating a child advocacy committee, or transporting low-income women to prenatal care appointments. Church members are also encouraged to commit to help children through individual acts of compassion and work for justice, whether volunteering as a tutor or responding to action alerts from a child advocacy organization.

The Children's Defense Fund (CDF) created the National Observance of Children's Sabbaths in 1992 as a way to coalesce child advocacy efforts across a broad range of religious traditions and amplify their voices in a united moral witness. Since then, hundreds of thousands of Children's Sabbath celebrations have been held across the country, most in individual congregations but some coordinated as community-wide, interfaith gatherings. CDF provides an annual Children's Sabbath Resource Manual with resources for planning, promotion, worship, lesson plans, advocacy activities, and follow-up.

The Children's Sabbath is just one of the ways that CDF partners with congregations and denominations to respond to Jesus' teaching that whoever welcomes one such child in his name welcomes him. "Congregations to Leave No Child Behind" (not connected with the legislation with a similar name) commit annually to conduct an educational event, provide a service ministry, engage in a spiritual discipline, or lead a Children's Sabbath service. CDF support to congregations includes circulating e-mail action alerts, providing contacts and resources for advocacy, conducting workshops, and speaking at religious gatherings.

Another resource to strengthen the justice work of congregations is the Samuel DeWitt Proctor Institute for Child Advocacy Ministry at CDF's Alex Haley Farm in Clinton, Tennessee. Participants in the five-day institutes leave renewed and better informed, equipped, and inspired to answer God's call to seek justice for the youngest and poorest among us. CDF has also cultivated Interfaith Child Advocacy Networks (ICAN) in a handful of cities to support coordinated, effective faith-based child advocacy. ICAN's grassroots activism is empowered by a broad interfaith network that shares program ideas and advocacy actions, breaking down the barriers that isolate congregations in their work on behalf of children.

Nearly twenty years ago, in partnership with CDF, a group of United Methodist women gathered at the Capitol in Washington, D.C., to urge passage of the Act for Better Child Care that was threatened with a presidential veto. They held aloft pictures drawn by children in church-housed child care programs. They presented then-President George H. Bush's domestic policy advisor with thousands of postcards calling for the passage of the child care act. The women seemingly had little in common. Some were young, some were old. Some were parents, some were single. Some were working, some were at home, and some were retired. They were black and white, Republican and Democrat. What united them was a bond of the Holy Spirit, the Advocate, who called them to live out their faith in a God of the last and the littlest.

The faith that called them into advocacy bore fruit when the Act for Better Child Care was signed into law and thousands of poor working parents could access quality child care. Their faith bore fruit in the lives of parents relieved of the awful choice between inferior child care they could afford and good care that depleted their money for food and other necessities. Their faith has borne fruit in the children, now grown to adulthood, who had a solid foundation of good care to prepare them for successful futures.

Confronted with the suffering of children, the first impulse of people of faith is typically to respond with direct service and acts of compassion. But the full biblical witness impels us to take to heart God's requirement in Micah 6:8 not only to "love kindness" but to "do justice." We act as Jesus' hands and feet and voice when we bind up the wounds of one child, but also when we urge new policies to address the 9 million children who lack health care coverage. We act as Jesus' hands and feet and voice when we prepare a meal for a poor family, but also when we advocate to change the systems that allow 13 million children to be at risk of hunger. In the words of Marian Wright Edelman, "Private charity is no substitute for public justice."

The religious community's leadership in achieving justice for children is a practical necessity and a moral imperative. No other institution has the capacity to achieve the social transformation needed for our nation to put children first. No other institution has its very fidelity and identity at greater stake than the Christian community that began with a poor homeless baby born to a teenage mother and that has been commanded to welcome the child.

Shannon Daley-Harris has served the Children's Defense Fund (www.childrensdefense.org) since 1990. During her tenure as director of religious affairs, she launched the National Observance of Children's Sabbaths and the Institute for Child Advocacy Ministry. She now advises CDF as a consultant for religious affairs.

9
Children in an Era of Welfare Reform
Sharon Parrott and Arloc Sherman

The story often told about the ten years that have passed since Congress enacted the 1996 welfare reform law[1] is a simple one: the number of families receiving cash assistance has declined, employment rates among single mothers have increased, and child poverty has declined. While these trends are real and important, it is also important to examine a broader set of trends to understand the full—and less encouraging—story.

■ *Child poverty has increased significantly since 2000.* Between 1993 and 2000, the share of the nation's children that were poor fell from 23 percent to 16 percent, a substantial improvement. But since 2000, some of that improvement has been lost, as child poverty rose to 18 percent in 2005. That is, between 2000 and 2005, the number of poor children went up by 1.3 million.

■ *Deep poverty has worsened as well.* Between 2000 and 2005, the number of children in families with cash incomes below *half* of the poverty line went up by more than 800,000.

■ *Employment rates among single mothers have fallen since 2000.* Between 1995 and 2000, the share of single mothers who were employed rose from 62 percent to 73 percent. But by 2005, their employment rates had retreated to 69 percent, undoing one-third of the earlier gains.

■ *The number of families receiving cash income assistance through the new welfare program called TANF (Temporary Assistance for Needy*

Families) shrank after 2000, even as the need for assistance grew. The number of families receiving cash assistance began falling prior to the 1996 welfare law, and the decline has been far greater than the decline in poverty. Caseloads continued to fall after 2000, even as poverty—and deep poverty—among children began to rise.

■ *TANF now helps a much smaller share of the families that are poor enough to qualify for the program than it used to.* Often overlooked in discussions about declining caseloads is the fact that more than half (57 percent) of the decline in TANF caseloads since 1996 is due to a decline in TANF participation by eligible families rather than to a reduction in the number of families that are poor enough to qualify for help. During the 1980s and early 1990s, about 80 percent of eligible families received cash assistance from AFDC, the program that preceded TANF. By 2003, under TANF, the figure was just 46 percent.

■ *A growing number of single mothers have neither jobs nor public cash assistance.* Between 1996 and 2004, the number of single mothers receiving TANF fell by 2 million, yet employment among single mothers rose by only about 1 million. This left a growing third group: jobless single mothers who receive no help from TANF or other major income support programs. From 1996 to 2003, the number of single mothers in an average month who were neither working nor receiving cash assistance from TANF or other programs—nor living with other individuals who had these sources of income—increased by 500,000 mothers with 1 million children. Most of these families have cash incomes below half of the poverty line.

An honest assessment of the first decade of welfare reform thus shows a mixed picture. In the 1990s, child poverty fell and employment among single mothers rose—both positive trends. Most analysts agree that these trends were the result of three factors: a strong economy that improved job prospects among low-skilled workers, better supports for low-income working families that improved work incentives and provided help (such as child-care assistance) to enable many single mothers to enter the workforce, and changes in state welfare policies to increase the focus on work. Even during this early period, however, a declining share of very poor families received basic income assistance from TANF.

After 2000, poverty began to rise and employment rates among single mothers fell—and the number of very poor families getting no help from TANF continued to grow. These families have missed out not only on basic income assistance but also on the employment-related help TANF can provide.

Studies have shown that many families have difficulty finding jobs because of serious barriers to employment such as mental and physical disabilities. A recent in-depth study of long-term TANF recipients in St. Paul, Minnesota found that a significant share had very low basic cognitive functioning, with IQs of 80 or less; some individuals could not read simple words, identify numbers, or tell time. Studies have also shown that parents who leave welfare for work often earn low wages and have unstable employment. To address these problems, a number of states have developed innovative programs designed to help recipients with the greatest barriers to employment prepare for and find jobs and to help recipients build their skills so they can obtain better jobs.

Changes in federal TANF policies enacted in 2006 could make it harder for states to operate welfare-reform programs tailored to recipients' needs. Those changes require states to place a much larger share of their TANF caseload in work activities and severely restrict the kinds of activities that can count toward federally imposed work requirements. Also, the new rules will make it harder for states to allow recipients to attend postsecondary education programs that last for more than twelve months. Some states have found such programs effective in helping recipients secure better-paying jobs with opportunities for advancement.

The cheapest and easiest way for a state to meet the new rules would be to assist fewer poor families, especially the families with barriers to employment who need the most help. Many states understand that taking such an approach would undermine their own goals of assisting poor families and helping them move to employment, so many state-level policymakers are trying to think creatively about how to meet the new federal requirements and serve families effectively. Still, the job of states is difficult, particularly since the new federal rules are not accompanied by any significant new resources. States' basic TANF block grant has not been adjusted since 1996 and has lost 22 percent of its value due to inflation. Yet Congress has extended the freeze on TANF funding through 2011. The continuing erosion in the value of the block grant will further encourage states to keep caseloads low.

Given these challenges, the real test of welfare reform over the next decade will be whether states and the federal government can improve on three fronts simultaneously: providing needed income support to the poorest children, helping those with the greatest problems find jobs, and helping those at the bottom rungs of the labor market gain desperately needed skills. Without progress in these areas, many very poor families will not get the help they need to make ends meet, and many poor and near-poor families might get by, but they will fail to improve their lives.

Sharon Parrott is director of the Welfare Reform and Income Support Division at the Center on Budget and Policy Priorities. Arloc Sherman is senior researcher at the center. For a more detailed analysis, see "TANF at 10: Program Results Are More Mixed Than Often Understood" by Sharon Parrott and Arloc Sherman (www.cbpp.org/8-17-06tanf.htm).

Note

1. For an overview of welfare reform, see Mark Greenberg et al., "The 1996 Welfare Law: Key Elements and Reauthorization Issues Affecting Children," *The Future of Children* vol. 12, no. 1 (Winter/Spring 2002), www.futureofchildren.org.

MINISTRY PROFILE
"The Children Are Not in the Way, They *Are* the Way": Youth in the Poor People's Economic Human Rights Campaign
Willie Baptist, Kristin Smith Nicely, and Blair Hyatt

The message of consumerism, individualism, and personal gratification that our society gives young people is radically different from the values Jesus taught. While growing up in such a culture can be confusing and often crippling, it is especially so for children living in poverty. Many poor youth face feelings of low self-worth, inadequacy, and a lack of control over their lives. They are confronted daily with messages that they are unworthy, unfit, and doomed for failure. Their poverty is portrayed as the fault of their parents, their communities, and themselves. Without material possessions, they become invisible at best, humiliated at worst.

The Poor People's Economic Human Rights Campaign (PPEHRC) and its educational arm, the University of the Poor, directly address our children's loss of their sense of community and their sense of self. Involvement in the Campaign increases feelings of self-esteem, connectedness, and community, while diminishing feelings of self-hatred, individualism, and isolation. Expanding young people's knowledge about poverty and its systemic roots results in their feeling stronger and better about themselves.

The Poor People's Economic Human Rights Campaign was formed in 1998, the fiftieth anniversary of the United Nations' Universal Declaration of Human Rights. It now consists of more than one hundred poor and homeless organizations from urban and rural areas of the United States. We were inspired religiously and organizationally to take up the mantle of the Reverend Dr. Martin Luther King Jr.'s Poor People's Campaign of 1968. In his campaign, people of all colors and ages, including children, took their places in what Dr. King called "the multiracial nonviolent army or 'freedom church' of the poor." Accordingly, our mission statement reads:

> The Poor People's Economic Human Rights Campaign is committed to uniting the poor across color lines as the leadership base for a broad movement to abolish poverty. We work to accomplish this through advancing economic human rights as named in the Universal Declaration of Human Rights, such as the rights to food, housing, health, education, communication and a living wage job.

The Bible has greatly shaped our values and views. Many young people maintain faith in Jesus and a deep belief that all human beings deserve the necessities of life. The PPEHRC respects that belief as a valuable gift and works to strengthen it. Following Jesus' teaching in Matthew 18:2-6, we aim to not offend children in any way and to make children central to our activities. (See "Children in the Poor People's Movement to End Poverty—A Movement That Plays Together Stays Together," found on www.universityofthepoor.org.)

One way we value youth is through our annual Youth and Parent Leadership School of the University of the Poor. The leadership school brings groups from across the county together to increase our knowledge, strengthen our relationships, and build our movement to end poverty. In 2006, a diverse group of young people, from eight to twenty years old, attended a youth track with workshops on economic human rights, leadership development, the PPEHRC, poverty myths, strategies to engage other youth, and approaches for organizing a social movement.

The youth began the week apprehensive and reluctant, their game faces on, and their cool firmly in place. As the discussions continued, the layers of self-protection began to chip away. Youth talked about the respect they held for their parents for their dedicated work with the campaign.

One of the most powerful discussions was on the misconceptions about poor people. Each youth expressed anger about how the poor are viewed and how people in their communities are treated. A young man cried while describing his mother's struggles to support her family. Another youth depicted the pressure he feels to help his mother's efforts to make ends meet. He divulged his feelings of guilt stemming from observing how hard she works to give him a better life, and his temptation to drop out of school to get a job to make things easier on his mother.

In the process of realizing and articulating feelings about being poor, youth began to free themselves of deep self-deprecation. Throughout the week, the young leaders gained a better understanding of the hardships they live with, the confusion they face, the faith they fear they will lose, and the difficulty of growing up poor in a materialistic society. At the conclusion of the week, the youth addressed the entire leadership school with a skit on the myths of poverty. Each member of the group spoke of change and community, of love and friendship, and of being blessed and unified. They found a process through which their voices could be heard and they learned not only how to fight back but how to fight together.

Besides the leadership school, the campaign has successfully held a number of children's press conferences after key events over the years (protests, tent cities, marches). These press conferences give young people the opportunity to speak to the media about the struggles they and their families are facing. Prior to these events, the youth are uncomfortable and wary, often embarrassed about the potential that their friends might see them on television. They wish that they could lie and pretend that they are not poor, hungry, homeless, and struggling to survive. But they face such feelings and speak out because they want all people to have a home, food, and health care. Often the stories they have to tell are so powerful that it is impossible to conclude without tears. After these conferences, the youth typically feel proud of themselves. They know they have accomplished something that was difficult and important for them to do.

The press conference format creates an environment in which youth may be taken seriously. People are more likely to listen to issues of poverty if they are being raised by young people. It is easier to blame an adult for struggling with poverty than to blame a ten-year-old. The young people see this and appreciate the important role they can fill in the campaign. They glimpse that they are valuable to God and to the community, not an unwanted statistic.

The challenge for our campaign, as for all people of faith, is that our work may reflect to children the truth that they are created in God's image. As we have stood firmly in the trenches with our children, the members of the Poor People's Economic Human Rights Campaign and the University of the Poor have evolved a saying that we believe corresponds with Jesus' view of children: "The children are not in the way, they *are* the way."

Formerly homeless father Willie Baptist is co-coordinator of the University of the Poor (www.universityofthepoor.org), education director of the Kensington Welfare Rights Union (www.kwru.org), and scholar in residence at Union Theological Seminary's Poverty Initiative (www.povertyinitiative.org). Kristin Smith Nicely manages a program for high-risk youth in Philadelphia. She is co-convener of the School of Youth and Parent Leadership at the University of the Poor and serves in the leadership of the Kensington Welfare Rights Union. Blair Hyatt is executive director of the Pennsylvania Head Start Association and assistant education director of Parent and Youth Leadership for the University of the Poor.

For more information about The Poor People's Economic Human Rights Campaign, see www.economichumanrights.org.

10
What Government Can (and Can't) Do
Curtis Ramsey-Lucas

According to the U.S. Census Bureau, 37 million people were living below the poverty level in 2005. This includes almost 13 million children, or nearly 18 percent of all children in the United States.[1] That's roughly one out of six children living in poverty.

Lest we think current poverty rates are merely the consequence of the soft economic recovery of recent years, we should note that in 1997—in the midst of a robust economy—nearly one in five children lived in poverty. The persistence of poverty, and in particular of children living in poverty, through good and bad economic times is a challenge that prompts the question: What can (and can't) government do to respond? Complicating matters is the fact that this question is raised in an environment of general skepticism regarding the efficacy of government programs to alleviate poverty. There is much government cannot do, yet this does not warrant the conclusion that there is little government *can* do.

As one example, we need only look at the history of Social Security and its success in reducing poverty rates among the elderly to see that government programs can be efficacious. More than seventy years ago, our nation made a commitment to address persistent poverty among the elderly through the creation of Social Security and, later, Medicare. That our nation has kept and largely succeeded at that commitment is evidenced by the sustained drop in poverty rates among the elderly. Without income from Social Security, nearly half of the elderly would be poor. With Social Security benefits, their poverty rate falls to approximately 10 percent.[2] That means roughly 12 million fewer elderly people live in poverty.

What then can government do to address child poverty?

First, government can adopt a more adequate standard by which to measure poverty. In medicine, the first step to successfully treating an illness is an accurate diagnosis. Likewise, in responding to poverty, government must first develop an accurate picture of the challenge it is confronting. In 2001, the Census Bureau recognized as much when it noted that "the official poverty measure should be interpreted as a statistical yardstick rather than a complete description of what families need to live."[3]

In 2007, the federal guidelines define poverty as an income below $17,170 for a family of three and below $20,650 for a family of four.[4] Granting that what people and families need to live varies from place to place, the official poverty measure is a remarkably conservative standard by which to measure the nature and extent of poverty in our society. Many people and families who do not fall below the official poverty threshold must yet make drastic choices each month between rent and food, healthcare and transportation.

As an alternative, thirty-four states and the District of Columbia now offer a self-sufficiency standard for income adequacy, a standard that more accurately reflects the income necessary to adequately meet basic household needs. The self-sufficiency standard incorporates living costs—food, shelter, health care, transportation, miscellaneous incidental necessities, taxes, and tax credits—and varies geographically, taking into account local differences in costs, which are considerable particularly in the areas of housing and child care.[5]

In addition to more accurately defining poverty, government can set clear and measurable goals in its efforts to reduce poverty. In 1999, Prime Minister Tony Blair introduced an initiative to end child poverty in the United Kingdom by 2020, with an initial goal of cutting it by one-quarter by April 2005. The British government designed a system to boost the incomes of working parents, including subsidies to low-wage workers and regular increases in the minimum wage. They established a ten-year strategy to increase access to quality, affordable child care and launched programs to develop healthy and school-ready preschoolers, teens, and young adults. These and other initiatives have yielded mixed results, and reforms continue. But setting a quantifiable agenda "focused the minds of politicians, the agencies and the public. Without it they would never have gotten as far as they have."[6] Despite missing its initial target, the British government reported a decline of 17 percent in the number of children living in poverty, some 700,000 children, from 2000 to 2005. By contrast, in the same period, the number of American children living in poverty has increased 12 percent.

One way that government can mitigate the effects of poverty is through a mix of programs of direct assistance and development. Three programs that have proven particularly effective in meeting the needs of children in poverty are the Special Supplemental Nutrition Program for Women, Infants, and Children (WIC), the free and reduced school lunch and breakfast programs, and Head Start.

WIC provides nutritious food, nutrition education, and access to health care for low-income pregnant women and children from birth to age six and their mothers who are at nutritional risk due to their household income. WIC has been credited with reducing low birth weights, child anemia, and infant mortality. In addition, WIC has been shown to reduce Medicaid costs for low-income infants and children. A 1992 Government Accounting Office analysis estimated that each $1.00 spent on WIC generated $2.89 in health care savings during the first year and $3.50 in savings over eighteen years.[7]

Good nutrition is an important factor in a child's ability to learn and perform in school. In 2004, 29 million children received meals through the National School Lunch Program. More than 4 billion lunches were served, with approximately 59 percent provided for free or at a reduced price. Following the program's inception in 1946, the program was expanded to include breakfast, given nutritional research that "eating breakfast increases standardized test scores, decreases behavior issues, and decreases absences and tardiness."[8] In 2004, more than 7 million children received a free or reduced-price breakfast each day through the National School Breakfast Program, enhancing their potential for academic success.

The Head Start Preschool Program is a comprehensive child development program serving children between the ages of three and five. Head Start provides free, comprehensive education, health, nutrition, and social services through local community-based organizations serving children and families. Launched in 1965, Head Start now serves nearly 1 million children. According to the U.S. Department of Health and Human Services, Head Start is effective in narrowing the education gap between disadvantaged children and other children. Once in kindergarten, Head Start graduates make substantial progress in vocabulary, math, and writing skills relative to national averages.[9] Additional studies confirm that children who have graduated from Head Start are less likely to repeat a grade, less likely to need special education, and more likely to graduate from high school.[10] These outcomes are significant for children in poverty given the links between education levels and future earnings. Head Start also provides the side benefit of a parental involvement component and employment for many low-income parents.

In addition to programs of direct assistance, government can address poverty through tax policy. Perhaps the clearest example of success in this regard is the Earned Income Tax Credit (EITC)—a tax credit for low-income working families, which now lifts more children out of poverty than any other government program. EITC provides tax reductions and wage supplements for low- to moderate-income working families. The federal tax system has included an EITC since 1975, with its latest expansion in 2001. More than 19 million federal income tax filers, roughly one out of every seven families who file, claim the federal EITC.

The federal EITC goes only to households with reported earnings under $35,458 (for two children in 2006). The size of the credit initially rises as earnings increase, with a cap at $4,300 for a family with two children and $2,604 for a family with one child; the credit then phases out gradually. The credit is phased out at a slightly higher income level for married couples than for other families. The EITC garners wide praise for its success in supporting work and reducing poverty. Census data show that in 2003, the federal EITC lifted 4.4 million people out of poverty, including 2.4 million children. The EITC has gained support across the political spectrum, with the backing of business groups as well as social service advocates.

The success of the federal EITC has led eighteen states and even three local governments to enact their own EITC that supplement the federal credit. Many state policymakers recognize the continuing importance of an EITC in difficult economic times. When unemployment rises or the real value of wages decline, state EITCs can help working families stay afloat. And when states are pushed to raise taxes in ways that may burden low-income families, state EITCs can relieve some of that burden.

Another potentially helpful tax policy that has been proposed is to provide a deduction for charitable contributions made by individuals who do not itemize deductions on their income tax returns, a group that includes more than two-thirds of taxpayers. Each year, this group of Americans contributes an estimated $36 billion to charities. Reinstating a limited deduction for nonitemizers would generate billions of dollars in increased giving to charities each year. Providing a deduction for charitable contributions has the double effect of providing additional support for charities while decreasing the tax burden on lower-to-moderate-income individuals who give a greater percentage of their incomes to charity.

Government will not have the resources necessary to adequately address persistent child poverty over the long term without rebalancing its priorities. Some reform and reallocation of the benefits government currently provides under Social Security and Medicare is essential in this regard. Projected federal spending on the elderly will rise from 8 percent of gross domestic product (GDP) to more than 10 percent by 2013. By contrast, unless dramatic changes are made to programs that benefit children, including the Temporary Assistance for Needy Families (TANF) welfare program, Medicaid, and federal aid to education, federal spending on children is projected to remain flat, at roughly 2 percent of GDP.[11] In our aging society, increasing numbers of people stand to gain from federal spending on the elderly, while the concerns of poor children remain more hidden. Without the political will to move beyond narrow self-interest, advocating for the needs of others beyond our immediate families, government will ultimately be frustrated in its efforts to address persistent poverty among our nation's children.

This reality points us toward consideration of what government cannot do to address persistent child poverty. Government can adopt a more adequate standard for determining the extent of poverty and can set clear and measurable goals for reducing child poverty. Government can help alleviate poverty among children through various assistance programs such as WIC, the free and reduced school lunch and breakfast programs, and Head Start, as well as TANF, the food stamp program, Medicaid, and the State Children's Health Insurance Program. Government can supplement incomes through such tax policies as the EITC and incentives to encourage charitable giving.

Where government is limited is in educating and inspiring people in their obligations to one another, directing their attention away from the self-interest and materialism inherent in a society that celebrates individual freedom. Individualism and material consumption go largely unchallenged by a false gospel of prosperity emanating from many pulpits. Where are the reminders that we are to look not only to our own interests but also to the interests of others (Philippians 2:4)? Who is sounding the call not to neglect to do good and to share what we have (Hebrews 13:16)? Such sacrifices, pleasing to God, are to characterize our life together as Christians. The reform of selfish desires influenced more by our society than the Spirit is an ongoing part of our walk with Christ, individually and as a corporate body.

Significant progress in reducing child poverty will require both government action and engagement from the private sector. The church must assume its proper role in promoting both. Advocacy of just public policies and direct assistance to those in need are essential. Equally if not more essential, however, is the church's potential to affect society by raising a people better able to live out the Great Commandment to love God and neighbor (Mark 12:29-31), to follow the Great Commission to make disciples of all nations and teach people God's ways (Matthew 28:18-20), to live up to the Great Criteria by meeting the needs of those with whom Christ most closely identifies (Matthew 25:31-46), and to resist the base materialism and self striving so pervasive in our society. This is not a work that can be accomplished by government. It is the calling of the church as it participates in God's work of personal and societal transformation.

Curtis Ramsey-Lucas is national coordinator of Public and Social Advocacy, National Ministries, American Baptist Churches USA (www.nationalministries.org), and editor of The Christian Citizen *magazine, a publication of National Ministries, American Baptist Churches USA.*

Notes

1. U.S. Census Bureau, "Income, Poverty, and Health Insurance Coverage in the United States: 2005," Current Population Reports, Series P60-231, 52.

2. Jared Bernstein and Mark Greenberg, "Lessons From the Social Security Debate," *The Nation*, April 26, 2005.

3. U.S. Census Bureau, "2001 Current Population Reports," Series P60-214, 5.

4. U.S. Department of Health and Human Services, "Annual Update of the HHS Poverty Guidelines," *Federal Register* 72, no. 15 (January 24, 2007).

5. Carol Goertzel, "From Poverty to Self Sufficiency—Dollars and Sense," *The Christian Citizen* 3 (2005).

6. Jared Bernstein and Mark Greenberg, "A Plan to End Child Poverty," *The Washington Post*, April 3, 2006.

7. United States Government Accounting Office, "Early Intervention: Federal Investments Like WIC Can Produce Savings" (Washington, DC: author, 1992), 23–24.

8. Bread for the World Institute, *Frontline Issues in Nutrition Assistance: Hunger Report* (2006), 55.

9. U.S. Department of Health and Human Services, "Head Start FACES 2000: A Whole Child Perspective on Program Performance" (Washington, DC: author).

10. W. S. Barnett, "Long-term Effects of Early Childhood Programs on Cognitive and School Outcomes," *The Future of Children* 5, no. 3 (winter 1995), 25–50.

11. "Generational Warfare," *The Washington Post*, December 9, 2003, A26.

MINISTRY PROFILE
Nueva Creación / New Creation Lutheran Church: Church and School Working Together for Kids
Heidi Unruh

A banner hanging in the sanctuary of the bilingual congregation Iglesia Luterana Nueva Creación/New Creation Lutheran Church depicts a dove hovering over a city skyline, with an affirmation of Jesus' mission: "The Spirit of the Lord has anointed us to preach good news to the poor . . ." New Creation's Philadelphia community cries out for good news. Generational poverty, family dysfunction, violence, and substance abuse plague the church's neighbors. A booming population of children and youth hunger for positive role models and productive activities.

Half a block from Nueva Creación is an elementary school with 1,100 children. In 1993, as part of the church-planting process, founding pastor Patrick Cabello Hansel networked with area residents and organizations to ask how the new church could serve its neighborhood. One of the first people he met was the principal of the elementary school. She invited him to speak at a parents' meeting, where he shared his hopes that the church could support the school. New Creation has fulfilled that promise in multiple ways.

The church shows its support by sponsoring special events for students around holidays, by hosting a thank-you breakfast for the staff and teachers of the school each spring, and by helping to keep the school grounds attractive. The wall around the schoolyard boasts a colorful mural of cheerful pictures and positive slogans, painted by Centro Nueva Creación's youth employment program. Tulips blossom in the school yard, thanks to another church-sponsored project. Church staff often have a presence on the campus as school lets out.

When students need academic help, school staff refer them to the after-school program at Centro Nueva Creación, which serves up to fifty children from kindergarten to sixth grade. After a snack, children do schoolwork for about an hour. Staff help supervise homework and give special attention to students struggling with reading. Children also learn a Bible verse every week, in exchange for tickets they can redeem for rewards. Most staff are bilingual, and the program celebrates holidays that honor the Puerto Rican background of many of the students.

The director of the after-school program helps families connect with other church programs, such as the food ministry. One of her goals is promoting greater parental involvement in children's education. "Parents don't know what they have. The schools belong to them. They have to take care of them, and use them to their advantage—to make them better." She observed that parental participation at school meetings was low because they were held during the day, and most parents in the neighborhood had to work. With city funds, she helped arrange for the school to add evening meetings. The church and community center provide space for parents' advisory meetings and were represented on a city-wide school improvement team.

The principal of the elementary school has been enthusiastic about the church's involvement. "Their after-school program is essential, both in terms of improving educational outcomes and in providing meaningful activities for kids." She noted that while there are legal issues to take into consideration with a church-school partnership, all parties involved have respected the appropriate boundaries. "The school and the church are both part of the community. You have to view kids in terms of their whole community context," she remarked. When church and school work together, the benefits flow to children and the community as a whole.

The story of Nueva Creación and other community-serving churches is told in Ronald J. Sider, Philip N. Olson, and Heidi Unruh, Churches That Make a Difference: Reaching Your Community with Good News and Good Works *(Grand Rapids: Baker, 2002). See the website www.centro nueva.org for more information and a youth photography exhibit.*

Jamal, age 9

SECTION III
Biblical Reflections on Children in Poverty

11

Jesus' View of Children

Wess Stafford with Dean Merrill

Jesus said, "Let the little children come to me, and do not hinder them" (Matthew 19:14; cf. Mark 10:14; Luke 18:16). His pronouncement has inspired painters, sculptors, poets, and songwriters down through the ages. The newsworthiness of this event is evident in the fact that all three Synoptic Gospel writers felt compelled to include it in their accounts of Jesus' life. Yet few expositors dwell on the strong word in Mark's account that when the children were being pushed aside, Jesus "was indignant" (Mark 10:14). Why did the Son of God get angry?

The religious leaders and Jesus were, at that moment, in the middle of discussing the important issue of divorce. The disciples felt this was no time for "irrelevant" children to appear on the scene and disrupt serious adult matters. I don't know how long Jesus tolerated the disciples' attempts at crowd control, but at some point he could stand it no longer. This powerful man, this brawny carpenter, raised his voice with great passion: "Let the little children come to me! Don't you dare hinder them! My kingdom belongs to such as these."

The children realized that this obviously in-charge adult was defending and protecting them, scolding adults on their behalf. Knowing they were loved and welcome, they came meekly at first, then boldly to him. He gathered them into his strong arms with a tender embrace. He placed his hands gently on them and breathed a blessing over them.

To understand Jesus' profound irritation that day, we must go back to an earlier conversation when he had made his Father's values about children perfectly clear. How could his disciples have forgotten such a vital lesson? How could they have missed the kingdom principle, "Children matter!"

It all began, according to the previous chapter (see Mark 9:33), with an ugly conversation on the road to Capernaum. Later on, Jesus called his disciples to account by saying, "What were you arguing about on the road?" Of course, none of them would repeat their words to Jesus; the text says, "They kept quiet" (Mark 9:34). But Jesus knew. They had been snarling at each other over status, namely, who among them was the greatest. All eyes were fixed on Jesus. Would he settle this pecking-order issue once and for all?

To the amazement of all, he called a little boy to come to him. Surely the disciples were perplexed and impatient. Nobody had given the boy's presence a second thought. To the disciples, he was just part of the scenery—invisible, unimportant. Some people still have an attitude that "children should be seen and not heard." The tragedy is that they are not only unheard but also unseen.

The child's sweet face must have provided Jesus with a momentary oasis of refreshment in the parched desert of grasping egos around him. Scripture tells us Jesus had this child stand in their midst. How long? Long enough for their eyes to fixate on him and for their mood to change as they silently studied his youthful spirit. Plucked from the fringes of power, he was suddenly front and center in the spotlight. What was Jesus trying to tell them?

At last Jesus spoke: "I tell you the truth, unless you change and become like little children, you will never enter the kingdom of heaven" (Matthew 18:3). And he could have added, "much less be the greatest in it!" The word "change" here is the same basic word that Peter used later on the day of Pentecost when he confronted the crowd on their role in crucifying the Son of God: "Repent, then, and turn to God, so that your sins may be wiped out" (Acts 3:19).

Jesus was not talking to his disciples about a minor modification, a slightly altered perspective. He was calling them to be radically overhauled from the inside out to be even a part of his kingdom, much less a leader. He might have added, "You demonstrated out there on the road that you have the child*ish* part perfected. But what you need is to become child*like*!"

By this he did not mean they had to become perfect. Sinful nature manifests itself in children as well as adults. This was not a lesson in somehow earning a place in heaven by appropriate behavior (i.e., by being "good children"). Jesus was speaking of humility. Lowliness of heart and mind. A teachable spirit. A willingness, even a delight, to learn. The kind of simple faith that wouldn't have walked tentatively on the water as Peter did but would have skipped and frolicked, completely secure in the Master's presence and protection. The trust that allows one to live contentedly by another's rules, even without fully understanding them. The need to love and be loved that simply cannot hold a grudge but is quick to forgive, confident that love can go on.

Jesus continued: "Therefore, whoever humbles himself like this child is the greatest in the kingdom of heaven" (Matthew 18:4). Up to this point Jesus had been talking about greatness in his kingdom, using the boy as an illustration. Now the child became the central focus as he forged ahead with renewed passion: "And whoever welcomes a little child like this in my name welcomes me" (Matthew 18:5). Mark takes it even a step further: "Whoever welcomes me does not welcome me but the one who sent me" (Mark 9:37).

Well, that certainly derailed the roadside debate! No doubt the disciples were stunned and reeling as Jesus' words sank in. An act of kindness to a child is the same as doing that act to Jesus Christ—indeed, to God himself?

One would think that a great new respect and appreciation for children would have seized their hearts. A whole new theology should have arisen that placed children at the center of the work of the church. A new priority for programs, budgets, and strategies should have been established that very moment. The words of Jesus couldn't have been any clearer. How unbelievable that they forgot all this within a few days. How unbelievably sad that the church would also forget it for the next two thousand years!

In Matthew 18:6, Jesus seems stricken with the potential for harm that awaits this little boy before him. He speaks in a somber tone: "But if anyone causes one of these little ones who believe in me to sin, it would be better for him to have a large millstone hung around his neck and to be drowned in the depths of the sea." He paints the most horrifying picture possible to drive home the seriousness of such an offense.

No doubt his mind raced with the many evils that history had perpetrated on little innocents, even the massacre of his Bethlehem peers after his birth. Next, he may have thought ahead to the coming harm of the child slave trade, child sexual exploitation, broken homes with fighting parents, child pornography, child soldiers, the scourge of AIDS. With a sob in his spirit, Jesus plunged on in his powerful teaching for three more verses, saying that if you are inclined to any of these despicable sins, it would be better for you to cut off your hand, lop off your foot, or gouge out your eye. Better to be maimed on earth than to be thrown into the eternal fire of hell!

And I'm sure the disciples agreed with him. Of course they would never deliberately hurt a child with such vicious sin, they told themselves.

But Jesus knew there was another whole side to the topic of children at risk. The sins that would break the heart of God didn't have to be sins of commission. Equally evil and far more prevalent in his kingdom would be sins of omission. Children could simply be considered unimportant, second-rate. Looking at the culture around him and, through time, to the present, Jesus was not willing to allow for that loophole. He pressed on in verse 10, "See that you do not look down on one of these little ones. For I tell you that their angels in heaven always see the face of my Father in heaven."

Now this was new territory. Don't even *look down on* these little ones? No society in history had given children equal footing to adults, and certainly not the dominant Roman or Jewish cultures of that day. But Jesus was talking about the values and passions of a new kingdom altogether—the kingdom these disciples were to proclaim.

I don't fully understand the pageantry and ceremonial worship that goes on in heaven. But from what Jesus said in Matthew 18:10, there exists in the midst of the elders and the heavenly hosts a cluster of angels—"their" angels—who are attuned to the needs of little children. Such is the influence, the access, the clout of children in the courts of heaven. I'm convinced that one of the most powerful forces on earth is the prayer of a child.

Jesus closes this discourse on the priorities of his kingdom with the well-known parable of the lost sheep. Many preachers say the point of this story is to illustrate the value of each individual to the Good

Shepherd, which is certainly true. You could get that generic application by reading the version in Luke 15:4-7. But here in Matthew 18, it is clear that Jesus is still talking specifically about his love for children. In verse 14 he concludes, "In the same way your Father in heaven is not willing that any of these little ones should be lost."

Soon afterward, Jesus and his disciples headed down the road toward Perea, a section east of the Jordan River, where "some Pharisees came to test him" (Matthew 19:3). Thus began the complicated discussion of divorce, with children and their mothers hanging around the fringes.

I can just picture the scene this particular day, Pharisees all around Jesus in the closest positions, with disciples in the next circle, leaning in to hear every momentous word. They still loved being in the proximity of power.

Then a little boy with a gap-toothed grin peeks out from behind the robe of Peter and gives Jesus a timid wave. A few feet away a little girl holds up a flower with a stem that is starting to bend over in the heat. Then baby, on his mother's back, coos and reaches out his chubby arms to the Master . . .

He, midsentence on the serious topic at hand, falters just a second; he winks at a mischievous little face. He raises his eyebrows to acknowledge the girl's flower, knowing that it is a gift for him. He can sense the love and admiration of the young mothers who wait patiently, still on the fringes.

Things are unraveling fast. The disciples feel responsible to regain order, lest this important dialogue get sidetracked. *There he goes again with kids,* they think. *Doesn't he realize the power and prestige of the men around him? This is a moment of high influence.* They start to stir, turning to motion with their hands and say: "Shhh!" with their lips. "Not now, ma'am. Can't you see the Master is occupied?" This is the poignant moment that Mark 10:14 reports, "When Jesus saw this, he was indignant."

The least of these—so easy to attack, so vulnerable, so unprotected— had, in a flash, been elevated to a place of significance and prominence, championed and shielded by God himself. In that moment it was abundantly clear that the disciples had been honoring the wrong people.

The next words were heard loudly and clearly by all: "Let the little children come to me, and do not hinder them." Jesus could have added, "Don't you remember anything from our discussion the other day? I told you as clearly and forcefully as anything I have ever taught you that the kingdom of God belongs to such as these." Even without such a scolding, I can picture the disciples, disarmed and deflated, watching in silence as an avalanche of triumphant little children surge past them into the embrace of their Master. Jesus instinctively takes them into his arms, hugs them tight, and blesses them. Giggles and laughter fill the air. Tears well up in the eyes of grateful young mothers.

Only one or two chapters later the Gospel writers tell us about Jesus' triumphal entry into Jerusalem. A large crowd—fathers, mothers, and children—line the streets to wave palm branches and shout in excited voices, "Hosanna to the Son of David! Blessed is he who comes in the name of the Lord!" (Matthew 21:9). Only a few people are irritated by this whole celebratory scene. "When the chief priests and the teachers of the law saw . . . the children shouting in the temple area, . . . they were indignant" (v. 15). Jesus immediately defended the young ones. He quoted Psalm 8:2: "From the lips of children and infants you have ordained praise."

At least the disciples kept quiet that day. Apparently they had finally learned what we all need to learn: children matter. Jesus will make time for a child regardless of what else is calling for his attention. He loves children passionately. They are too precious to hurt and are right at the center of God's heart and kingdom.

Dr. Wess Stafford has served as president of Compassion International (www.compassion.com) since 1993 and hosts a national radio program, Speak Up with Compassion®. *Dean Merrill is an author, former magazine editor, and ordained minister. This chapter is adapted with permission from Wess Stafford with Dean Merrill,* Too Small to Ignore: Why Children Are the Next Big Thing *(Colorado Springs, Colo.: Waterbrook Press, 2005), 197–210. Scripture references in this chapter are from the* New International Version.

MINISTRY PROFILE
Cookman Alternative School for At-risk Youth
Jill Witmer Sinha

The motto of the youth leaders at Cookman United Methodist Church is "Youth ministry is when youth begin to do ministry." Pastor Donna Jones credits much of the success of her congregation's work with youth to their strategy of drawing on young people as collaborators. In the late 1990s, several young adult members envisioned safe havens for youth. They recognized that many teens in the church's inner-city North Philadelphia neighborhood, lacking adult supervision and meaningful activities, could easily drift into negative behaviors such as truancy or misdemeanors or remain safe but isolated indoors. The young adults dreamed with the church of comfortable, safe, cool places where community youth could come to hang out, do homework, play video games, and maybe experience the Christian faith in a relevant and unobtrusive way. After this vision was presented to the North Philadelphia Cluster of United Methodist Churches, six churches developed Teen Lounges.

The Teen Lounges became an integral part of the cluster's alternative education program, which grew out of a network of care and connections. Through a relationship with the University of Pennsylvania, Cookman participated in a research project that uncovered the breadth and complexity of devastating issues confronting youth in their community, including violence, trauma from abuse, family conflict, and an escalating school drop-out rate. In 2002, up to half of Philadelphia public high school students were at risk for truancy, and 1,100 truant youth were referred for public services. In response, the North Philadelphia cluster churches broadened the scope of their services to youth with a publicly funded alternative school.

The program has been serving about sixty youth per year since 2003. It provides truant youth with academic support, as well as a range of developmental options, including a weekend retreat, child care, computer repair training, and participation in a community-based arts program. The program allows older students to complete coursework independently while attending to work and family responsibilities. Participants gain opportunities to form healthy relationships with other youth and with caring, Christian adults.

The students enrolled in this alternative education program are representative of many poor urban youth: all had dropped out of high school; more than one-third were offenders; one-fourth had used or sold drugs; reading skills ranged from second- to fourth-grade level; more than one-third were parents or had been pregnant; a third had mental health issues; four had received public assistance; nine had been homeless. Interviews with students in the program reveal a disturbing picture of their experiences in prior educational environments: frequent fights with other students, negative influences from peers who skip school, needing to be constantly on their guard, feeling disrespected and neglected by teachers. One youth used the phrase "fear and hatred" in describing the atmosphere at his high school.

Yet students in Cookman's program attended more than three days a week on average. Students received individualized attention and described the classroom setting as "more relaxed and fun." One youth appreciated that the teachers "stop and help you" when you need it and that the teachers cared "whether you get it." Youth affirmed that the staff and teachers cared about them outside of the program. On several occasions, for example, teachers and church members provided transportation and helped youth find housing. Students also felt that they trusted the staff and could talk to them if they had personal issues.

One of the most dramatic signs of a positive peer culture at this program was the lack of fighting. Almost every youth who enrolled had been in fights, both verbal and physical, with other youth or teachers in their previous school environment. At this program, these same youth talked about being able to get along better and having made good friends due to the smaller size of the program. There was only one violent incident that involved damaged property during the year-long case study.

The program has reinforced the educational aspirations of teens who previously did not expect to graduate or go on to college. One youth said that she had been active in extracurricular clubs such as debate and the softball team in her regular high school, yet she felt there was no one in her life who seemed interested in her or proud of all that she was doing. She quit school in her senior year. Now, with the support of Cookman's program, this young woman completed her GED and started taking college courses. She volunteers with the program and is a natural cheerleader for other youth.

Cookman gives youth and young adults a voice in the education program through a Student Youth Board. The church's young adults have also formed a nonprofit organization called Emerging Ministries Corporation (EMC). Through EMC, young members in the congregation who show leadership potential gain experience as part-time instructors in the alternative education program or become peer counselors. These youth also help train other adults to relate to urban adolescents in effective ways.

The effect of Cookman's journey with neighborhood youth can be measured not only in educational outcomes but also in relational and spiritual support. Although the curriculum includes no religious instruction or formal religious activity, staff may offer to pray for students or talk about their own beliefs. Youth in the education program and the Teen Lounges are invited to church-sponsored activities, such as Bible studies, retreats, and movie nights. Regular participants in the Teen Lounges credited their involvement as contributing to their positive outcomes such as being less likely to get pregnant or get high, being challenged to start over, and being more involved in church activities. About a third of the students participating in the alternative education program have visited or attended a church.

What is remarkable about Cookman's engagement with at-risk youth is that Cookman is a "little itty bitty church," in the words of one of its members. Its membership is currently around 120, with the majority of members under twenty-five years of age. The congregation has not incorporated a separate nonprofit and has always collaborated with other organizations as a strategy, acknowledging that they could never do this level of work on their own. Cookman's ministry has been funded through a mix of federal, state, city, denominational, and private monies. By recognizing the potential of youth and working collaboratively to help them achieve their dreams, Cookman has demonstrated that even small churches can make a big difference.

Jill Witmer Sinha, PhD, is assistant professor with the School of Social Work at Rutgers, The State University of New Jersey. Dr. Sinha conducted research on Cookman's program through a grant from the Department of Health and Human Services, Administration for Children and Family, through the Compassion Capital initiative.

12
Why and How Christians Should Care for Poor Children
Ronald J. Sider and Heidi Unruh

An astounding 210 verses in the New International Version of the Bible refer to those who are "poor" or "oppressed." If our churches featured this theme with the same prevalence and passion as Scripture, how might God use the church to bring new hope to children in poverty?

God's Special Concern for the Poor

God loves all people equally. Yet the special place in God's heart for the poor and vulnerable is evident throughout the Bible (e.g., Leviticus 23:22; Psalm 12:5; 140:12; 146:7-9; Proverbs 19:17; 21:13; Isaiah 3:14-15; 25:4; Zechariah 7:9-10; Luke 1:52-53; James 2:5). God's compassion is most evident in tender attentiveness toward poor women and children: "You shall not abuse any widow or orphan. If you do abuse them, when they cry out to me, I will surely heed their cry" (Exodus 22:22-23). God hears the cry of Ishmael, son of Hagar, Abraham's abandoned and abused second wife, when they are near death in the wilderness (Genesis 21:17)—a plea for help that echoes in the experience of many poor children today.

God intervenes to uphold the cause of those who are impoverished and mistreated, as promised in 1 Samuel 2:8: "He raises up the poor from the dust; he lifts the needy from the ash heap." The Bible also teaches that God sometimes judges and brings down the rich. Mary's Magnificat points to the social reversal associated with Jesus' incarnation: God "has filled the hungry with good things, and sent the rich away empty" (Luke 1:53). Later, Jesus preached, "Woe to you who are rich!" (Luke 6:24).

Yet it is not riches alone that provokes God's wrath, but two dangers associated with wealth. First, Scripture harshly warns those who acquire wealth by exploiting the poor. "You who make iniquitous decrees . . . that widows may be your spoil, and that you may make the orphans your prey! What will you do on the day of punishment?" (Isaiah 10:1-3; see also Isaiah 3:14-15, Amos 2:7, Micah 2:1-5). Second, God's anger is also aroused by people who have plenty, yet neglect the needy. In Ezekiel 16:49, God proclaims regarding the destruction of the city of Sodom: "This was the guilt of your sister Sodom: she and her daughters had pride, excess of food, and prosperous ease, but did not aid the poor and needy" (see also Luke 16:19-31). In God's eyes, ignoring the needs of the poorest is as grievous as idolatry and sexual abominations.

The biblical record demonstrates that ultimately, God judges societies by how they treat the people at the bottom. That is how much God cares for the poor.

Sharing God's Heart for "The Least of These"

In response to poverty and in contrast to the ways of the world, the Scriptures repeatedly instruct God's people to embrace compassion and justice (Exodus 23:6; Leviticus 19:10; Proverbs 14:21; Psalm 41:1; 112:9; Amos 5:11-14; Micah 6:8; Romans 12:13; 2 Corinthians 8:10-15; Galatians 2:10; Ephesians 4:28; James 2:14-16). After the Exodus, the Lord commands the Israelites not to treat widows, orphans, and foreigners the way they had been treated by the Egyptians. Instead, God's people are to love those on the margins, just as God has rescued them (Deuteronomy 15:15). God's people are to seek the welfare of their community (Jeremiah 29:7) and to become a source of blessing to all people (Genesis 12:3).

God identifies with the poor so strongly that caring for them is a way of expressing our love for God. "Whoever is kind to the poor lends to the LORD" (Proverbs 19:17), but "those who oppress the poor insult their Maker" (Proverbs 14:31). This theme reappears in Jesus' parable of the sheep and goats (Matthew 25:31-46). Jesus surprises the righteous with his insistence that they had fed and clothed him: "Just as you did it to one of the least of these who are members of my family, you did it to me." Since Jesus names the poor as part of his family, followers of Jesus are to show care to the poor and neglected as if they were serving the Savior.

Because compassion is a fundamental aspect of God's character, there is a connection between knowing and loving God and serving those in need (see Deuteronomy 10:17-20; Proverbs 14:31; 29:7; Isaiah 58:6-8; Ezekiel 16:49-50; 18:5-9; Matthew 22:37-39; 2 Corinthians 8:1-9; James 1:27; 1 John 3:17). In Jeremiah 22:16, God commends the upright king Josiah: "He defended the cause of the poor and needy; then, it was well. Is not this to know me? says the LORD." Bryant Myers summarizes this connection: "Loving God and loving our neighbor are two sides of the same gospel coin. They are inseparable, seamlessly related. . . . At the end of the day, how we treat the poor is a measure of whom we truly worship."[1]

Concern for the Poor in Jesus' Teaching and Example

Jesus demonstrated his Father's compassion for the poor and vulnerable in his teachings (Matthew 25:31-46; Mark 10:21; Luke 6:20-21; 10:25-37; 12:33-34; 14:12-14) and by his example (Matthew 9:35-36; 20:30-34; Mark 8:1-8; Luke 7:22; John 13:29).

In Luke 4:16-21, Jesus announced his mission by quoting from Isaiah 61:1: "The Spirit of the Lord is upon me, because he has anointed me to bring good news to the poor. He has sent me to proclaim release to the captives and recovery of sight to the blind, to let the oppressed go free, to proclaim the year of the Lord's favor." Jesus lived out this mission by teaching, healing, and breaking the oppression of evil (Matthew 9:35). He showed special attention to those on the social margins: women, children, the disabled, and the outcasts. Jesus' teachings underscored the dangers of captivity to wealth and the blessedness of a life open to the needs of others.

After his resurrection, Jesus empowered his disciples to carry on this mission (John 20:21). We too are empowered by the Spirit of Christ to bring good news to the poor.

What Can God's People Do?

Matthew 26:6-13 tells the story of a woman who anointed Jesus with costly perfume. When the disciples protested that the perfume should rather have been sold and given to the poor, Jesus defended the woman's actions, saying, "You always have the poor with you."

Some have taken this statement to mean that social ministry is ultimately futile and that Christians should concentrate on saving souls. But it is important to understand Jesus' words in the context of the passage in Deuteronomy to which he was referring: "There will always be poor people in the land. Therefore I command you to be openhanded toward your brothers and toward the poor and needy in your land" (Deuteronomy 15:11, NIV). Jesus' words do not justify sidelining poverty and focusing on the world to come. Rather, the overwhelming reality of poverty in this world is an urgent call for people of faith to open their hands freely to those in need.

The Bible indicates seven broad pathways of action in response to poverty. Whatever our course of action, we are to immerse our ministry in prayer, serving in "the strength that God supplies, so that God may be glorified in all things through Jesus Christ" (1 Peter 4:11). And we must work persistently, trusting that "in the Lord [our] labor is not in vain" (1 Corinthians 15:58).

1. *Practice hospitality, live in solidarity.* The starting point is to make our homes places of refuge and care for neighbors in need (Proverbs 31:20; Romans 12:13; 1 Timothy 5:10) and to make all people, regardless of economic status, feel welcome in our congregations (James 2:2-4). But who are our neighbors? Do our lives bring us alongside those who are suffering, or do they remain "out of sight, out of mind"? The incarnational ministry of relocation follows Jesus' example: "The Word became flesh and lived among us" (John 1:14). We can show solidarity with poor children by choosing to dwell, work, shop, and make

friends in their communities. Saying to those who are poor, "Your people shall be my people" (Ruth 1:16) gives us a personal stake in their well-being.

2. *Share resources.* The early church practiced Jesus' teaching to give to the poor (Luke 6:30) by sharing with all who had need (Acts 2:44-45) and by taking a collection for famine relief (Romans 15:26; 2 Corinthians 8:1–9:15). In view of God's mercy (Deuteronomy 15:15), God's people are commanded to make their resources generously available to the poor: "Do not be hard-hearted or tight-fisted toward your needy neighbor. You should rather open your hand, willingly lending enough to meet the need" (Deuteronomy 15:7-8).

While this passage calls for voluntary charity, other passages point to more institutionalized mechanisms for caring for those unable to provide for themselves. For example, every third year, the people's tithe was to go to support poor widows, orphans, and foreigners as well as the Levites (Deuteronomy 14:28-29; 26:12). Individuals, churches, and the nation as a whole all share responsibility for the welfare of society's most vulnerable members.

Scripture consistently reminds us that our compassion toward others is a reflection of God's compassion for us. Whatever we give to others, we can never match God's generosity in sending Christ while we were yet sinners (Romans 5:8; 2 Corinthians 8:7-9).

3. *Empower self-sufficiency.* One key way in which the law of Moses directed resource owners—which in ancient Israel meant landowners—to aid those in need was through the practice of gleaning. "When you reap your harvest in your field and forget a sheaf in the field, you shall not go back to get it; it shall be left for the alien, the orphan, and the widow, so that the LORD your God may bless you in all your undertakings" (Deuteronomy 24:19-20; see also Exodus 23:10-11). The story of Ruth shows the model of gleaning in action (Ruth 2:8-17). By putting others' needs ahead of his profit, Boaz kept a young widow's family from starvation.

As Amy Sherman points out, a core principle of gleaning is that it "gives the able-bodied poor an opportunity to meet their own needs through their own application of labor."[2] Benevolence should affirm the connection between work and self-sufficiency. Whenever possible, Christian charity should affirm the dignity of those who are poor by creating opportunities for them to provide for themselves and their families, rather than perpetuating crippling dependency.

4. *Invest in development.* Internal or external barriers may hinder people from meeting this biblical goal of self-sufficiency. Development means generating change within people or their environment that brings life in the community closer to God's ideal. Isaiah 61:3-4 identifies the goals of development:

> To provide for those who mourn in Zion—to give them a garland instead of ashes, the oil of gladness instead of mourning, the mantle of praise instead of a faint spirit. They will be called oaks of righteousness, the planting of the LORD, to display his glory. They shall build up the ancient ruins, they shall raise up the former devastations; they shall repair the ruined cities, the devastations of many generations.

The first goal is personal transformation, helping people develop the character, identity, attitude, and skills necessary to overcome the obstacles in their path. The call in Romans 12:2 to "be transformed by the renewing of your minds" produces change from the inside out. The second goal is community development that renews the institutions, infrastructure, economy, and environment of a healthy community. As Isaiah 58:12 promises, "You shall be called the repairer of the breach, the restorer of streets to live in." Community development looks beyond individual well-being to lay a foundation of wholeness that can endure for "many generations."

5. *Promote justice.* Because "the LORD loves justice" (Psalm 37:28), people of God are likewise called to "do justice" (Micah 6:8), particularly on behalf of the powerless (Deuteronomy 10:17-19). "Speak out for those who cannot speak, for the rights of all the destitute. . . . Defend the rights of the poor and needy" (Proverbs 31:8-9).

Many biblical texts call on political rulers to use their power to deliver the needy and oppressed (see Psalm 82:3-4; Proverbs 29:4; Jeremiah

22:2-3; 23:5; Daniel 4:27). Psalm 72 describes the role of the king in advancing justice: "May he judge your people with righteousness, and your poor with justice. . . . For he delivers the needy when they call, the poor and those who have no helper" (Psalm 72:2, 12). When selfish, powerful people deprive others of their rightful access to productive resources, the state must use its power to intervene. When individuals and institutions in the community do not or cannot provide security or basic necessities for "those who have no helper," government has a God-given responsibility to save lives.

If government and other sectors of society fail to uphold justice, God's people are to hold them accountable. The prophets confronted political leaders who oppressed the poor and failed to protect the vulnerable. Isaiah 10:1-2, for example, challenges rulers who use crooked laws to "make the orphans your prey" (see also Jeremiah 5:26-28; 22:13-17; Ezekiel 22:23-30; Micah 7:3). The prophets also confronted business leaders engaged in immoral and exploitative practices that hurt poor families (see Nehemiah 5:1-13; Jeremiah 22:13; Hosea 12:7-8; Amos 8:4-6; Micah 2:1-2; 6:10-12). Jesus likewise spoke out against respected religious leaders who kept the letter of the law but neglected justice and mercy, and who out of greed would "devour widows' houses" (Matthew 23:23; Luke 20:46-47). Promoting justice means protecting the vulnerable from those who abuse political, economic, or religious power, as well as bringing victims of injustice to the attention of those with the power to defend their cause.

6. *Break the cycle of poverty.* The most radical concept in the Hebraic economic system was the year of Jubilee. Every seven years, all debts were to be canceled (Deuteronomy 15:1-2). The fiftieth year was a special Jubilee, in which all land was to be returned to its original owners: "You shall proclaim liberty throughout the land to all its inhabitants. It shall be a jubilee for you: you shall return, every one of you, to your property and . . . to your family" (Leviticus 25:10).

This passage recognizes the self-perpetuating nature of wealth and poverty. Originally, the land was divided equitably among extended Israelite families. Over time, families that experienced a loss of resources became vulnerable to moneylenders, large land owners, and powerful civic leaders who could take advantage of their struggle for survival. Families who fell into debt or lost their land passed these liabilities on to their children. The year of Jubilee represented liberation from this downward spiral, bringing fresh opportunities and hope to each generation.[3] Children would not be hostage to the sins of their parents. (See also Ezekiel 18:2-4 on this principle.)

The policy of Jubilee reflects the biblical ideal that in a healthy society, each family has the freedom and capacity to earn its own living and to participate with dignity in the life of the community. Because of human sinfulness and the fallen state of the world, however, people fall into the downward cycles of poverty and dependency. God's plan is that society be structured in a way that gives each generation the chance to break free from the limitations of the past.

7. *Share good news with the poor.* Jesus' first sermon announced that "the year of the Lord's favor," or Jubilee, had arrived (Luke 4:21). Like the year of Jubilee, the coming of Christ means good news to the poor and liberty to those in bondage—whether trapped by oppressive systems, disease and disability, unjust treatment at the hands of others, or their own sinful choices. In Jesus' ministry, spiritual, physical, social, and economic liberation go hand in hand.

Followers of Christ can proclaim the good news that those who are financially poor may be wealthy in spirit (Luke 6:20; see also Proverbs 15:16; 16:8, 19; 28:6; Luke 21:1-4; 2 Corinthians 6:10; 8:2, 9). As James 2:5 points out, "Has not God chosen the poor in the world to be rich in faith?" The gospel is good news as well to those who are poor in terms of power and prestige. In contrast to the low standing of children in society, Jesus declares that they occupy a special place in God's kingdom (Luke 18:16).

We also share good news with the poor and vulnerable when we affirm that they are created in God's image (Genesis 1:26), treat them with dignity and respect (Luke 18:35-42), and value their contributions (Luke 21:1-4). As the story of Peter and John's encounter with the beggar at the temple illustrates, we can extend people spiritual care and fellowship even when giving financial resources is not possible or appropriate (Acts 3:3-11).

Conclusion

People who love God can disagree on many points of public policy and social welfare. There can be no room for debate, however, on the Bible's claim on Christians to care for the poor as a central expression of our faith.[4] If we do not share God's passion to uplift the poor, we cannot claim to know God in a biblical way. "How does God's love abide in anyone who has the world's goods and sees a brother or sister in need and yet refuses help?" (1 John 3:17).

It is important not to be misunderstood. We dare not reduce knowing God to a concern for social justice. Nor can we earn our way into heaven by caring for the poor. The only assurance of salvation is to cling to the cross, trusting God to forgive us for Jesus' sake. While God shows special concern for the vulnerable, God does not care more about the salvation of the poor than the rich. Jesus confronted the poor along with the wealthy for their sins. In fact, Scripture specifically forbids us to be partial to the poor (Leviticus 19:5).

When it came to children, however, Jesus' arms were open wide. His instructions were clear: "Whoever welcomes one such child in my name welcomes me" (Matthew 18:3). Our love of Jesus is to find tangible expression in the way we treat children. Jesus' condemnation of those who abuse children was equally clear: "It would be better for you if a great millstone were fastened around your neck and you were drowned in the depth of the sea" (Matthew 18:6). Neglecting the needs of poor children is a form of giving them offense (James 2:15-16).

If we love Jesus and seek to conform our lives to Scripture, we will care for children wounded by poverty—physically, emotionally, and spiritually—and promote a society that shares resources to meet their needs. We will prayerfully intervene to break the yoke of generational poverty and create fresh opportunities for families to develop self-sufficiency. We will protect children and their families from exploitation and advocate their cause to those in power. And we will offer children and their families the hope of our faith in Christ, who shared in their poverty during his sojourn on earth so that through him all might live in abundance (2 Corinthians 8:9).

Ronald J. Sider is founder and president of Evangelicals for Social Action (www.esa-online.org), director of the Sider Center on Ministry and Public Policy, and professor of theology, holistic ministry, and public policy at Palmer Seminary in Wynnewood, Pennsylvania. As a writer and consultant on church-based social ministry, Heidi Unruh directs the Congregations, Community Outreach, and Leadership Development Project, and serves as staff associate with Evangelicals for Social Action.

Notes

1. Bryant Myers, "Isaiah, Which Is It?" (retrieved from www.network935.org).

2. Amy Sherman, *ABCs of Community Ministry* (Hudson Institute, 2001), 13.

3. Ronald J. Sider, *Just Generosity* (Grand Rapids: Baker, 1999), 65–67.

4. For a more developed presentation of this claim, see Ronald J. Sider, *Good News and Good Works: A Theology for the Whole Gospel* (Grand Rapids: Baker, 1999).

Poetry by Youth Growing Up in Poverty

Unknown Life

Violence is nothin like silence
Anger, rage I wish there could
 be a brighter day
Gangs, most of them slang
But it's normal when you live
 around it for so long
Da shooting goes on and on
Da killin won't ever be gone
It's crazy but it won't faze me
I look up to da Lord to recreate
 me
Cuz I'm tired of livin these ghetto
 fantasies
They affect me in every way
I try to stay away but I can't
Cuz it's around everyday

Sonya (age 15) The poets in these features are youth participants in Neighborhood Ministries (www.neighborhoodministries.org), which cares for the physical, emotional, mental, and spiritual needs of at-risk children and their families in Phoenix. The Neighborhood Ministries Art Center offers kids opportunities in the arts by providing relationships with artist mentors, art-based activity classes, and involvement in Dream Projects. Poems were collected by Art Center director Noel Barto.

13
Slipping Off on the Bible's Sloping Side
Charles E. Poole

Three years ago I left the pastorate of a wonderful congregation to become an inner-city minister with the LifeShare Foundation, a charitable foundation with the mission "to meet unmet needs in the lives of Mississippi's most at-risk and underprivileged children." In my work as the LifeShare community minister, I pay pastoral visits to the homes of families in Jackson who are living in difficult circumstances and, with the resources of the foundation, provide help with specific needs. That help is often as small as diapers, occasionally as large as refrigerators or beds. We give grocery store gift cards or purchase food for hungry families, and we partner with families in paying utility bills to keep or restore light, heat, and water in the home.

All of this is done in the context of pastoral conversation and prayer in the homes of those we help. In most cases, I visit the homes on a regular basis. Additionally, I teach after-school Bible classes for children and teens in some of our city's most low-income urban apartment complexes. At those gatherings we pray, learn Bible verses, and talk about God, life, and right and wrong. We also eat lots of cookies and drink lots of juice.

Every now and then, someone will ask me, "Why? Why would you leave the 'normal' pastorate for this unusual ministry among families and children in difficult places?" The answers to such questions are never simple. What we church folk refer to as a call is wrapped in quiet mystery that runs deeper than words.

Having acknowledged that, I do have a rather simple answer to "Why?" My answer is that I sort of slipped off on the Bible's sloping side.

Even if you place a perfectly smooth Bible on an even table on a flat floor in a level building, the Bible will still tilt in the direction of whoever is most powerless, most voiceless, invisible, small, and poor. Here are a few of the high points on the Bible's sloping side:

If you lend money to my people, to the poor among you, . . . you shall not exact interest from them. (Exodus 22:25)

When you reap the harvest of your land, you shall not reap to the very edges of your field, or gather the gleanings of your harvest. (Leviticus 19:9)

Do not be hard-hearted or tight-fisted toward your needy neighbor. . . . Open your hand to the poor. (Deuteronomy 15:7, 11)

Those who mock the poor insult their Maker. (Proverbs 17:5)

Share your bread with the hungry; . . . when you see the naked, [clothe] them. (Isaiah 58:7)

How great are your sins, you who . . . push aside the needy. (Amos 5:12)

Go, sell your possessions, and give the money to the poor . . . ; then come, follow me. (Matthew 19:21)

The Spirit of the Lord is upon me, because he has anointed me to bring good news to the poor. (Luke 4:18)

Give to everyone who begs from you. (Luke 6:30)

When you give a banquet, invite the poor, the crippled, the lame, and the blind. (Luke 14:13)

How does God's love abide in anyone who has this world's goods and sees a brother or sister in need and yet refuses to help? (1 John 3:17)

That's just a small handful out of a huge armful of verses about the call of God to care for the weak, the sick, the small, the outcast, the poor. The Bible always tilts in their direction.

So it is no surprise that every now and then some Christians lose their balance and slip off on the Bible's sloping side, the side which leans in the direction of whomever has the smallest voice, the hardest struggle, and the least power. It is, as they say, a very slippery slope.

Charles E. Poole serves with LifeShare Foundation in Jackson, Mississippi (www.lifesharefoundation.org). Before becoming their community minister in 2003, he was a pastor for twenty-six years.

MINISTRY PROFILE
Churches, Homeless Single Mothers, and Professionals: Three-way Partnerships That Build a Bridge of Hope for Children
Leslie Homer-Cattell

St. Timothy's Episcopal Church in Cincinnati has a child-friendly reputation in the community. So when their Bridge of Hope mentoring group saw how the once-homeless family they were matched with was struggling, it was natural that they thought of the children.

"Kelly[1] is a typical fifteen-year-old girl—independent minded but still very much a child," says Theresa Prewitt, one of the mentors. "She went through some really rough times and hit rock bottom. We put our heads together with her mom, Jen, and asked, 'What is Kelly passionate about? What would inspire her?'"

After learning from Jen that Kelly loves to sing, the mentors found singing lessons at the local college. One couple offered to make the lessons possible; other mentors helped with transportation. This church-based mentoring group and formerly homeless mother teamed up to make sure daughter Kelly had something positive to work toward.

The mentors from St. Timothy's reached out in friendship to Jen, her seven-year-old, Isaac, and four-year-old, Jeffrey, too. Theresa invited them to join her, her husband, and their three sons at soccer games and a water park and to go out for ice cream. Later she invited Jen's family to the church's St. Nick Dinner and then to the Palm Saturday event for children.

Jen's boys started coming to church with Theresa's family on Sundays, too. Isaac began going up with Theresa during communion for the priest's special blessing for children: "Jesus loves you so much." On Easter, Jen brought all three children to what she started calling "our church." When Jen had questions about baptism, Theresa referred her to the priest.

"St. Timothy's really embraced this family!" says Liz Rand, staff person for Bridge of Hope Clermont and Eastern Hamilton Counties (Ohio). "Now they have a new community of support."

Ending and Preventing Homelessness . . . One Church and One Family at a Time

The conviction that a community of supportive friends from one church can make a lasting, multigenerational difference in the lives of one homeless single mother and her children was the vision of Bridge of Hope's founders, Linda Witmer and Sandy Lewis—a public health nurse and a women's shelter director. At their invitation, thirty-seven Christians gathered in a Pennsylvania church basement in March 1987 to hear three homeless mothers share their stories.

"There was a strong sense of hope and optimism at that meeting," says Andy Leatherman, former pastor of what is now Sandy Hill Community Church, where the meeting was held. "What gripped people was the idea that churches could be involved in meeting homeless families' needs. Many of us had the story of the sheep and the goats on our minds. That was the theological underpinning—Jesus' words to help the poor and love others. This was not about 'rescuing' people; it was more about simply loving them."

Those present represented a cross section of different Christian churches, but a deep sense of Christ's call to compassion united them. Some of those gathered went on to develop Bridge of Hope's program model: a three-way partnership between one homeless or at-risk family, one trained church-based mentoring group, and professional staff. The first homeless single mother and her infant daughter were matched with a mentoring group in December 1989.

Clear Roles, Clear Goals

The role of each partner in Bridge of Hope's model is clearly defined. The Bridge of Hope mentoring group builds supportive friendships with one single mother and her children and provides the kind of practical assistance friends give one another, such as help on moving day, occasional childcare, or a meal to share. In addition, these eight to twelve people from one church model healthy parenting and other life skills and nurture the family's spiritual growth through prayer, natural sharing of their own faith journeys, and invitations to church functions.

Bridge of Hope's professionally qualified social-service staff train and support mentors as they engage with families on their journey toward wholeness. In addition, staff members assist the mother with goal setting, budgeting, and developing other life skills. Rental assistance is also provided on a decreasing basis to allow time for the job training and personal growth that will help the woman to get on her feet and stay there for the long haul.

The single mother in Bridge of Hope works toward financial self-sufficiency for herself and her children through full-time employment. She focuses on meeting her goals and managing a budget. She develops friendships with her mentors.

The four goals of Bridge of Hope's three-way partnership are clearly defined, too. Over the period of the twelve to eighteen months that the family is in the program, single mothers aim to attain permanent housing; financial self sufficiency through employment; increased self-esteem and growth in areas of holistic living; and life-changing friendships that continue after the woman graduates.

More than 80 percent of single mothers in Bridge of Hope successfully establish a secure home, a circle of supportive friends, and a plan for long-term economic stability and success for their families.

Exemplifying Christ's Love

After more than a decade of successful ministry and in response to inquiries from across the country, Bridge of Hope National was founded in 2002 to end and prevent homelessness for women and children across the United States by calling churches into action. The nonprofit's mission is equipping compassionate Christians to exemplify Christ's love to homeless mothers and children by using the Bridge of Hope model to connect these families with churches in their communities.

"For children in Bridge of Hope who were once homeless, seeing the church as a place of belonging comes through in mentoring friendships," says executive director Edith Yoder. "Bridge of Hope provides a clear second-generation impact—not only in long-term stability and safety but also in creating this place of belonging which is vital for children."

For Theresa and the other mentors from St. Timothy's, exemplifying Christ's love to a once homeless family has been a rewarding experience. "I will not be able to say goodbye to this family when Jen graduates from Bridge of Hope," says Theresa. "I've told her that I'm a permanent fixture—as long as she wants me in her life, I'm there! This family has a community beyond what they had before. And I couldn't imagine life without these four people."

Leslie Homer-Cattell is director of outreach and communications for Bridge of Hope National (866-670-HOPE, www.bridgeofhopeinc.org).

Note
1. The names of the mother and children in this story were changed to protect their privacy.

14
Children in the Early Church
James Riley Estep Jr.

The Christian community of the second and third centuries A.D. valued the life and well-being of children from any economic class but took particular interest in the underprivileged. In Roman culture, children were valued primarily due to socioeconomic reasons. This is not to suggest that parents did not love their children, but children were primarily seen as heirs (cf. Galatians 4:1-7), a means of continuing the family name and economic endeavors. The typical family structure, with the father as undisputed head of the household (Ephesians 6:1-3; Colossians 3:18-20) was reflective of the notions of *patria potestas* (Latin, father authority) and the *paterfamilias* (Latin, father of family) pervasive throughout Roman society.[1] The familial hierarchical structure reflected in the New Testament conformed to the cultural expectation of the times.[2]

In Roman culture, the father was principally responsible for the provision, education, and economic well-being of children. However, the law also gave fathers absolute authority over their children and household, including the killing or abandonment of newborns.[3] W. V. Harris is author of a seminal article documenting the historical practice of child *expositio* (i.e., exposure, the leaving of children to the elements, often leading to their death). He explains that while parents engaged in this brutal but legal practice for a number of reasons, "the commonest reasons for exposing infants were probably economic ones."[4]

The Christian community responded to such treatment of underprivileged or unwanted children in two ways: opposition to the practice of child infanticide and *expositio*, and a commitment to adopting orphans. These Christian measures to counteract the marginalization and even

144

extermination of children in Roman culture have ongoing applicability for the church.

Opposition to Infanticide and Expositio

The *Didache* 2.2, one of the earliest extrabiblical Christian documents, proscribers, "You shall not kill a child in the womb, nor shall you slay it when born." The opposition to this practice drew not only on the value of life but also on the Christian community's commitment "on behalf of the downtrodden," with the *Didache's* treatment of child exposure "immediately followed by a focus on sins against the poor and needy."[5]

Justin Martyr, an early Christian scholar of the mid second century, penned a protracted verbal objection to the practice of child exposure, stating that the act itself was immoral and that it could lead to the prostitution and/or death of an innocent child.[6] Tertullian, an early third century scholar from North Africa, made a similar argument.[7] In that same time period, the scholar Clement of Alexandria contended that the practice of *expositio* was pagan in practice and due to "licentious indulgence,"[8] as did Athenagoras, one of the first Christian philosophers.[9] At the beginning of the fourth century, Lactantius linked the idea of family poverty and the practice of *expositio*, noting some parents hoped for the children to be rescued by others.[10] Some early Christian literature censured such parents as condemned to divine retribution.

Opposition to the practice of infanticide and/or *expositio* was almost always linked to objections to the practice of abortion, which also was often associated with the parents' impoverished circumstances.[11] In spite of the church's unanimous and persistent opposition to these practices, they continued into the medieval period.[12]

Care for Orphaned Children

The call to concern for widows and orphans expressed in James 1:27 was institutionalized by the ante-Nicene church. The Shepherd of Hermas, a second-century book of instruction, directs readers:

Having fulfilled what is written, in the day on which you fast you will taste nothing but bread and water; and having reckoned up the price of the dishes of that day which you intended to have eaten, you will give it to a widow, or an orphan, or to some person in want, and thus you will exhibit humility of mind, so that he who has received benefit from your humility may fill his own soul, and pray for you to the Lord.[13]

The *Didascalia Apostolorum*, a third-century Syrian Christian document, speaks to the care of widows and orphans. The responsibility for orphans falls to the bishop, who is instructed to "bestow care upon these," but also to provide for widows who "are in need of help through want or sickness or the rearing of children."[14] It details the care to be provided to orphans:[15]

1. Childless Christian adults should adopt male or female orphans.
2. Christian parents of a son should adopt a female orphan to be his wife "when her time is come."
3. Adopted male orphans should "learn a craft" so as to become a productive member of society once grown.
4. In both instances, male or female orphans are to be adopted so as to not place "a burden upon the love of the brethren."
5. No one receiving church support due to being an orphan should be shamed, "for he is esteemed at the altar of God, therefore shall he be honoured of God."

Such endeavors for orphans are first mentioned in the time of Arian bishop George of Cappadocia (361) but probably existed earlier.[16]

It was expected that Christian parents would provide instruction in the faith to their children (Ephesians 6:1, 4; Colossians 3:20-21), supported by leaders of the Christian community (Titus 1:6-9; 1 Timothy 3:4-5).[17] Orphans, having no parents, would not have such opportunities unless Christian adults adopted them. Thus care for orphans was a means of bringing children into the faith and of expanding opportunities to provide ongoing Christian instruction.

Conclusion

The contemporary Christian community must maintain its historical commitment to homeless and abandoned children. The practices of infanticide and *expositio* are still present throughout the world today, particularly in countries suffering from extreme poverty or recovering from disaster and conflict. However, even in the United States such practices are not unknown. Media reports circulate all too often about abandoned children, deserted in an alley or hospital, or the intentional demise of an unwanted child. Churches can respond by taking a stand opposing harm to children, whether the abuse is physical or psychological, and promoting the adoption of children without parents. This role is still as vital today as it was centuries ago.

Dr. James Riley Estep Jr. is professor of Christian education at Lincoln Christian Seminary (Lincoln, Illinois).

Notes

1. See D. L. Stamp, "Children in Late Antiquity," in *Dictionary of New Testament Backgrounds* (Downers Grove, IL: InterVarsity Press, 2000), 197.

2. W. A. Strange, *Children in the Early Church* (Eugene, OR: Wipf and Stock, 1996), 77.

3. Gillian Clark, "The Fathers and the Children," in *The Church and Childhood, Studies in Church History* 31, ed. Diana Wood (Cambridge, MA: Blackwell, 1994), 5.

4. W. V. Harris, "Child-Exposure in the Roman Empire," *The Journal of Roman Studies* 84 (1994): 15. The other reasons given for child exposure were deformity, illegitimacy, and superstition (e.g., evil omens).

5. O. M. Bakke, *When Children Became People*, trans. Brian McNeil (Minneapolis: Fortress, 2005), 115; cf. Didache 5.2.

6. 1 *Apology* 27, 29.

7. *Apology* 9.7, 8, 17.

8. Clement of Alexandria *Stromata* 2.18.

9. *Legatio* 35.6.

10. *Divine Institutes* 6.20.

11. See Bakke, 114–28; Strange, 78–79.

12. Rob Meens, "Children and Confession in the Early Middle Ages," in *The Church and Childhood*, Studies in Church History 31, Diana Wood ed. (Cambridge, MA: Blackwell, 1994), 57, 92–93.

13. *Similitudes* 3.

14. *Didascalia Apostolorum* 14.

15. Ibid., 17.4.1–3.

16. *Ecclesiastical History* 2.28; cf. Timothy S. Miller, *The Orphans of Byzantium: Child Welfare in the Christian Empire* (New York: Catholic University of America Press, 2003), 46.

17. See Judith M. Gundry-Volf, "The Least and the Greatest: Children in the New Testament," in *The Child in Christian Thought* (Grand Rapids: Eerdmans, 2001), 58–59. *Didascala Apostolorum* 4 makes instruction of children mandatory for those aspiring to become bishops.

MINISTRY PROFILE
Mentoring That Makes a Difference:
Three National Models
Heidi Unruh

Do you have an hour a week to make a difference in a child's life? Mentoring has been demonstrated to have a significant positive impact on at-risk youth. Research on Big Brothers Big Sisters found that after eighteen months of a mentoring relationship, children were:

- 46 percent less likely to begin using illegal drugs
- 27 percent less likely to begin using alcohol
- 52 percent less likely to skip school
- more confident of their performance in school
- more likely to get along better with their families and peers[1]

The following profiles provide a snapshot of three excellent national programs that can help connect churches and individuals with mentoring opportunities.

Big Brothers Big Sisters

Program information Big Brothers Big Sisters (BBBS) matches children ages six through eighteen with mentors in one-to-one relationships. Most children come from low-income households, and many live in families with histories of substance abuse and/or domestic violence. Once a week, Bigs and Littles meet to share a fun activity or to hang out at the child's school. BBBS screens and trains mentors, matches Bigs and Littles based on personalities and preferences, and provides ongoing support to the relationship. The Hispanic Mentoring Initiative emphasizes a connection with Hispanic communities and the recruitment of Latino Bigs and Littles.

Story[2] "I thank God for giving me the opportunity to meet someone like Joe. I am truly blessed to have him in my life."

Those are the words of Little Brother Aldo, who today is a confident college student pursuing his dreams—and building his future. But it wasn't that long ago that Aldo's future didn't seem so assured. He had entered a "rough spot" in his life, and he was feeling down on himself.

That's when Big Brother Joe stepped in. Joe encouraged Aldo to participate in the activities he enjoyed most: music, baseball, after-school programs, and community service. The more Joe encouraged Aldo to believe in himself and strive for excellence, the better Aldo felt about himself, and the better he did in school. The hard work paid off!

As Aldo will be the first to tell you, the benefits of mentoring last a lifetime. "My Big Brother has been there for me when I needed him most. Now we hang out whenever we can. Not as Big and Little . . . but as lifelong friends."

Contact Big Brothers Big Sisters National Office, 215-567-7000, www.bbbs.org

Amachi

Program information The most isolated and at-risk children in the United States are the estimated 7.3 million children who have an incarcerated parent or parents. Without effective intervention, 70 percent of these children will likely follow their parent's path into jail or prison. The Amachi mentoring program was developed to provide the children with an alternative path by establishing the consistent presence of loving, caring people of faith.

Amachi, a West African word that means "who knows what God has brought us through this child," connects children of prisoners with mentors recruited through local congregations. Children meet weekly with their Amachi mentors, who often live and worship in the same neighborhoods as the children. The church provides a meeting ground, while an onsite coordinator provides ongoing volunteer support.

Amachi's goal is that one-to-one mentoring by caring adults will significantly improve the life opportunities of the children. Who knows what God will bring us through this ministry?

Story[3] Lisa Thorpe-Vaughn, executive director of Amachi Pittsburgh at the Pittsburgh Leadership Foundation (PLF), knows from firsthand experience the benefits of mentoring children of incarcerated parents. For seven years, Thorpe-Vaughn has been mentoring her now twenty-one-year-old mentee, whose father was incarcerated.

"It's unbelievable," said Thorpe-Vaughn. "I thought she would have never made it. The fact that she made it out of high school was significant enough for me." At one point, Thorpe-Vaughn spent a whole year trying to get her mentee back in school, as she had been expelled for fighting from every school she attended. The hard work paid off. Today the mentee is serving as a mentor herself, is a VISTA worker for the Amachi program, and is enrolled in ministry school through her church. "To really see her giving back because someone stopped and gave her some time makes this all worthwhile," said Thorpe-Vaughn.

Contact Amachi Program, Public/Private Ventures, 215-557-4418, www.amachimentoring.org

Kids Hope USA

Program information Kids Hope USA builds caring relationships . . . one child, one hour, one church, one school at a time.

One child, one hour is the heart of Kids Hope USA: one caring adult mentoring an at-risk child one hour every week. When kids feel loved and valued, they are better able to learn, grow, and succeed. But one church, one school is what makes the program unique. Churches are well-positioned to recruit mentors who will be faithful over the long haul. Schools appreciate the program because it meets an urgent need.

Kids Hope USA brings churches, schools, volunteers, and at-risk students together. A church approaches a local elementary school with the offer of partnership through an in-school mentoring program. Kids Hope USA trains a part-time paid director and mentors from the congregation. Mentors commit to meeting weekly with one student for one hour at the school. Beyond the academic assistance, the investment of time offers the potential for lasting friendships to form, creating a platform for emotional and social growth. As one pastor remarked, "If there is any ministry we undertake at our church that embodies the Easter message of God's power to renew and give hope, Kids Hope USA has to be it."

Story[4] The principal told Janet that Steve was the worst bully at school when she became his Kids Hope USA mentor. She was told that he terrorized the other kids on the playground. Steve was quite different from Janet. He came from a poor white family that placed little emphasis on reading and expressed strong feelings about police and African Americans. Janet was a middle-class African American female who valued reading and worked as a federal probation officer.

Within six weeks, Steve stopped his aggressive behavior and asked the principal if he could be a peer mediator, a role that would allow him to help other kids avoid fights. He needed extra help with his reading, so Janet visited the school twice each week. They began working together at his home, where Steve's family always welcomed his mentor.

The one-to-one relationship changed Steve, but it touched Janet's life as well. She was so moved by the impact that God could have through her that she left her job as a probation officer to enroll in seminary.

Contact Kids Hope USA, 616-546-3580, www.kidshopeusa.org

Notes

1. J. P. Tierney, J. B. Grossman, and N. L. Resch, *Making a Difference: An Impact Study of Big Brothers Big Sisters* (Philadelphia: Public/Private Ventures, 1995).

2. From the Big Brothers Big Sisters website, www.bbbs.org/site/c.diJKKYPLJvH/b.1755227/k.A872/Real_Life_Stories/apps/nl/newsletter.asp.

3. From the Amachi website, "Pittsburgh Uses Innovative Approaches to Locate Children" (fall 2004), www.amachimentoring.org/pittsburgh.htm. /

4. From the Kids Hope USA website, www.kidshopeusa.org. The names in the story have been changed. See also www.centeronfic.org/v2/stories/kids_hope.html and the chapter on Kids Hope USA in *Street Saints*, by Barbara Elliott (Radnor, PA: Templeton Foundation Press, 2004).

15
Gifts from Ministry with the Poor
Amy L. Sherman

God is passionate for the poor and vulnerable. There is a special place in God's heart for children. And God would have the church imitate these concerns. The abundance of Scripture verses on justice and compassion should be sufficient, but God does give us an additional motivation: When we in love pursue our neighbors' welfare, we are ourselves enriched. God promises incredible blessings and rewards for our obedience.

These blessings come to us only through an entanglement of our lives with the lives of people in need. Often the church has been guilty of a cheap benevolence that wants only to help the poor but isn't willing to know them. The good Samaritan did not toss canned goods and a tract at the wounded traveler along the Jericho road; he dirtied his hands as he bandaged the man's wounds. True mercy is, as church father Gregory of Nyssa taught many centuries ago, "a voluntary sorrow that joins itself to the suffering of another."

The six gifts described below are not gained from contact with poor children and their families that is cold, distant, and sterile but through ministry that is relational and holistic.

The Gift of Agitation

Abundance and affluence anesthetize us. It is easy to grow comfortable with this world that we are supposed to see as a place of pilgrimage and not as our true home. But when we allow ourselves to be touched by the brokenness and pain of others, then an oh-so-needed holy discontent

begins to grow within us. As we entangle our lives with those who suffer, we begin to become agitated with the ways things are. There's not
supposed to be discrimination. There's not supposed to be child abuse.
There's not supposed to be hunger, privation, and despair.

We are spiritually impoverished by an absence of agitation. We need
the holy discontent we can gain by participating in the sufferings of our
neighbors.

The Gift of Growth in Humility and Dependence on God

When we are engaged in friendships with hurting, struggling people, we
become aware of their overwhelming needs and of our desperate need
for God to intervene. The reality of inadequacy is a great gift for all who
are proud and self-reliant. It is when we are weak that Christ's strength
is perfected in us.

The feeling of being overwhelmed produces true humility. We begin to
think first of our need for Jesus, rather than focusing with false confidence on the resources we have to offer to those who are hurting. The
four friends of the paralytic in Mark 2 did not look at their friend and
think, *We can fix him.* Rather, the only thing they knew to do was to
carry their friend to Jesus. It is a gift to be reminded of our limits so that
we can cast ourselves upon a limitless God.

The Gift of Learning About the Nature of True Faith

People with support networks, IRAs, savings accounts, and educational
degrees have safety nets to depend on. When those in more marginalized positions pray, "God, give me my daily bread," there is an authen-
ticity about their dependence. There is a sense, "If God doesn't come
through, I'm sunk." This dependency of the believing poor on God is
good for us to witness. "Listen, my beloved brothers and sisters. Has not
God chosen the poor in the world to be rich in faith?" (James 2:5). Some
Christians who are economically poor have a great gift of faith. We benefit by learning from the immediacy and urgency of their relationship
with God.

The Gift of Aroma

The service of the church is different from that offered by the government or by secular nonprofit organizations. Christians must display merciful servanthood that stands out as being not indigenous to the human heart but implanted by the Holy Spirit.

Our compassionate ministries become a tangible witness to the reality of God and God's love when those ministries have the look, feel, and smell of God about them. This happens when we minister as Jesus, the bread of life, ministered—to the whole person. A cheap benevolence that lacks the aroma of the bread of life will not often get noticed by unbelievers. When the world looks at our compassionate ministries, they should be intrigued. We demonstrate the presence of God through a relational, holistic ministry that transforms people's lives. And that witness goes out before a watching—and sniffing—world and draws unbelievers to Christ.

The Gift of the Garden

We are promised the gift of the garden by God in Isaiah 58:10-11 (NIV):

> If you spend yourselves in behalf of the hungry and satisfy the needs of the oppressed, then your light will rise in the darkness, and your night will become like the noonday. The LORD will guide you always; he will satisfy your needs in a sun-scorched land and will strengthen your frame. You will be like a well-watered garden, like a spring whose waters never fail.

The word translated "spend" (v. 10) connotes the idea of issuing forth or pouring out mercy. These are terms used to talk about water. We are asked to spend ourselves—our time, our heart, our very souls. We are to pour out this "water," to issue it forth to water others.

Are we fearful that by pouring ourselves out, we ourselves will become empty and dry? The promise of Isaiah 58:11 is that when we share life-giving water in sun-scorched places among those who are thirsty, we will not run dry. God pours himself and his provision into us, so that we become like a well-watered garden. God's Spirit will never fail us.

The Gift of Invigorated Worship

Our vision of God enlarges as we begin to witness God acting in other people's lives. We see new facets of who God is as we witness all his deeds. Ministry gives us the gift of insight into God's character in ways that we may have otherwise missed.

For invigorated worship, middle-class Christians need to mingle with people whose prayer requests may be different from their own—for example, prayers of children related to abuse or discrimination, or being placed in foster care, or having to work while trying to finish high school. When we are in relationships with families who are praying for God's deliverance out of difficult circumstances and then witness God answer those prayers, we see more clearly the multifaceted grace and provision of our heavenly Father. Our adoration of God is deepened, and our worship is enriched.

Conclusion: The Gift That Keeps Giving

Perceiving and celebrating the gifts that accompany ministry with poor children and their families has the additional benefit of helping the church to see them as contributors rather than mere receivers. Our relationship becomes one of mutual appreciation and respect. The gospel we proclaim not only saves people from negative things; it saves them for positive things. Thus we can share the gift of the joy of giving.

Dr. Amy L. Sherman is senior fellow at the Sagamore Institute, where she directs the Faith in Communities Initiative (www.centeronfic.org). This chapter is reprinted with permission from Amy Sherman, "Loving Our Neighbor's Welfare," Enrichment *(spring 2004): 51–56.*

Epilogue: A Personal Word on Hope
Heidi Unruh

For the needy shall not always be forgotten, nor the hope of the poor perish forever. (Psalm 9:18)

When I was in seventh grade, I marched in a winter parade with other youth from my Christian school, shivering as we sang, "Jesus loves the little children, all the children of the world."

What does it mean today to affirm that "Jesus loves the little children" when little children are suffering from deprivation and despair? What evidence or assurance can we offer? On what grounds do we claim to have hope?

This book provides factual information, a theological foundation, and stories of compassion in action to inspire a compelling vision of how we can make a difference for children in poverty. But my motivation is more personal. I have hope because I grew up as a poor child.

I remember using a bucket to pour water taken from a neighbor's tap to flush our toilet when our water was shut off. I remember using the oven for heat and candles for light when the electricity was shut off. I remember moving into friends' homes, cramped trailers, and even more-crowded motel rooms when we didn't have money for rent. I remember the local elementary school refusing to enroll my siblings because we didn't have a permanent home address. I remember searching the house for spare change to buy groceries. I remember the almost-stale taste of food-pantry bread and the almost-spoiled taste of food-pantry meat. I remember the shame of wearing school clothes that didn't quite fit me, or fit in.

And I remember my mother calling churches when we found ourselves stranded in a strange town, our car out of gas, on our way to another city where my stepfather had been promised work. In the difficult time after the work did not materialize, I recall that money, food, and even a place to live appeared without fanfare, thanks largely to Christians who heard of our predicament. And I can never forget the joy of sharing what little we had with others in the same situation and seeing God miraculously provide enough to go around.

I have hope, because experience has taught me that poverty cannot keep from children the gifts of life that matter most: the love of family, the warmth of community, the blessedness of sharing, the confidence of belonging to God.

In response to the challenges posed by this book, one of the most important first steps you can take is to get to know a poor child and her or his family. See them not as problems to be solved or cases to be managed but as people to befriend and enjoy. Let your life become entangled with their lives. You don't have to have the right answers or the right resources. You just need to come with a welcoming heart, and let yourself be guided by the simple assurance of the familiar song: "Little ones to him belong; they are weak, but he is strong."

Benediction: A Child's Prayer

Marian Wright Edelman

Child:
All you who are dreamers, too,
Help me make our world anew.
I reach out my dreams to you.

Reader:
Let us go forth to make the world safe
    for the dreams of children;
may we be partners in manifesting
    God's promised new creation
    of compassion and justice.
Amen.

Reprinted with permission from Marian Wright Edelman, Guide My Feet: Prayers and Meditations on Loving and Working for Children *(Boston: Beacon Hill Press, 1995), 188.*

Appendix A
Resources for Information and Action

Books

Understanding Child Poverty

Nancy Boxill, ed., *Homeless Children: The Watchers and the Waiters* (Binghampton, NY: Haworth Press, 1990).

Children's Defense Fund, *Wasting America's Future* (Boston: Beacon, 1994).

Pamela Couture, *Seeing Children, Seeing God: A Practical Theology of Children and Poverty* (Nashville: Abingdon, 2000).

Lisa Dodson, *Don't Call Us Out of Name: The Untold Lives of Women and Girls in Poor America* (Boston: Beacon Press, 1999).

Aletha C. Huston, ed., *Children in Poverty* (New York: Cambridge University Press, 1991).

Jonathan Kozol, *Amazing Grace: The Lives of Children and the Conscience of a Nation*, 2nd ed. (New York: Harper Perenniel, 1996).

Susan E. Mayer, *What Money Can't Buy: Family Income and Children's Life Chances* (Cambridge, MA: Harvard University Press, 1997).

Virginia E. Schein, *Working from the Margins: Voices of Mothers in Poverty* (Ithaca, NY: Cornell University Press, 1995).

Arloc Sherman, *Poverty Matters: The Cost of Child Poverty in America* (Washington, DC: Children's Defense Fund, 1997).

Mobilizing the Church to Respond to Poverty

Larry K. Brendtro, Martin Brokenleg, and Steve Van Bockern, *Reclaiming Youth at Risk: Our Hope for the Future*, revised edition (Bloomington, IN: Solution Tree, 2002).

Victor Claman and David Butler with Jessica Boyatt, *Acting on Your*

Faith: Congregations Making a Difference, A Guide to Success in Service and Social Action (Boston: Insights, 1994).

Shannon Daley and Kathleen Guy, *Welcome the Child: A Child Advocacy Guide for Churches* (New York: Friendship Press and Children's Defense Fund, 1994).

Bill Ehlig and Ruby Payne, *What Every Church Member Should Know About Poverty* (Highlands, TX: Aha! Process, 1999).

Jan Johnson, *Growing Compassionate Kids: Helping Kids See Beyond Their Backyard* (Nashville: Upper Room, 2001).

Tim Keller, *Ministries of Mercy: The Call of the Jericho Road* (Phillipsburg, NJ: P&R, 1989).

Robert Lupton, *Compassion, Justice, and the Christian Life: Rethinking Ministry to the Poor* (Ventura, CA: Regal Books, 2007).

Kenneth Miller and Mary Wilson, *The Church That Cares: Identifying and Responding to Needs in Your Community* (Valley Forge, PA: Judson Press, 1985).

John Perkins, ed., *Restoring At-Risk Communities: Doing It Together and Doing It Right* (Grand Rapids: Baker, 1995).

Willie Richardson, *Reclaiming the Urban Family: How to Mobilize the Church as a Family Center* (Grand Rapids: Zondervan, 1996).

Jolene L. Roehlkepartain, *Teaching Kids to Care and Share* (Nashville: Abingdon, 2000).

Rick Rusaw and Eric Swanson, *The Externally Focused Church* (Loveland, CO: Group, 2004).

Cheryl Sanders, *Ministry at the Margins* (Downers Grove, IL: InterVarsity Press, 1997).

Amy L. Sherman, *The ABCs of Community Ministry: A Curriculum for Congregations* (Washington, DC: Hudson Institute, 2001).

Ronald J. Sider, *Just Generosity: A New Vision for Overcoming Poverty in America* (Grand Rapids: Baker, 1999).

Ronald J. Sider, Phil Olson, and Heidi Rolland Unruh, *Churches That Make a Difference: Reaching Your Community with Good News and Good Works* (Grand Rapids: Baker, 2002).

Jay Van Groningen, *Communities First* (Grand Rapids: CRWRC, 2005).

Organizations and Websites

Information and Policy Analysis on Children in Poverty

Call to Renewal (calltorenewal.org)

Catholic Campaign for Human Development (povertyusa.org)

Center on Budget and Policy Priorities (cbpp.org)

Child Welfare Information Gateway (childwelfare.gov)

Forum on Child and Family Statistics (childstats.gov)

The Future of Children, Princeton-Brookings (futureofchildren.org)

Kids Count Census Data, Annie E. Casey Foundation
  (aecf.org/kidscount/census/)

National Black Child Development Institute (nbcdi.org)

The National Center for Children in Poverty (nccp.org)

Poor People's Economic Human Rights Campaign
  (economichumanrights.org)

Search Institute (searchinstitute.org)

Urban Institute (urban.org/cnp)

Advocacy and Ministry with Children in Poverty

Bread for the World (bread.org)

Bridge of Hope (bridgeofhopeinc.org)

Center for Family and Community Ministries (baylor.edu/CFCM/)

Center on Faith in Communities (centeronfic.org)

Children in Poverty Initiative, National Ministries, American
  Baptist Churches USA (nationalministries.org/CIP/)

Children's Defense Fund (childrensdefense.org)

Children's Hunger Fund (childrenshungerfund.org)

Christian Community Development Association (ccda.org)

Christian Volunteering (christianvolunteering.org)

Christians Supporting Community Organizing (cscoweb.org)

Congregational Resource Guide (congregationalresources.org)

Devos Urban Leadership Initiative (devosurbanleadership.org)

ELCA Women and Children Living in Poverty program
  (elca.org/dcs/wclip.html)

Ele:Vate (elevateurbanyouth.org)

Faith in Action (putyourfaithinaction.org)

Faith and Service Technical Education Network (FASTEN)
  (fastennetwork.org)
Family and Children Faith Coalition (fcfcfl.org)
JustFaith Ministries (justfaith.org)
Love INC (Love in the Name of Christ) (loveinc.org)
Network 9:35, Evangelicals for Social Action (network935.org)
New Focus (newfocus.org)
Reclaiming Youth Network (reclaiming.com)
Save the Children USA (savethechildren.org)
S.A.Y. (Save America's Youth) Yes! (sayyescenters.org)
Urban Ministry (urbanministry.org)
Voices for America's Children (voicesforamericaschildren.org)
World Vision U.S. Programs (worldvision.org)

Appendix B
What Can We Do?
Identifying Ministry Opportunities

Learn to do good; seek justice, rescue the oppressed, defend the orphan.
(Isaiah 1:17)

God is inviting you to "learn to do good." What can you and your church do to help poor children achieve their potential and experience God's good design for their lives?

Just as the needs are great, the possibilities for ministry are endless. No one can do everything . . . but we are all called to do something. The following exercises can help you identify forms of response that are timely, practical, and relevant for your context. The first exercise relates to personal or household service; the second to church-sponsored programs; the third, a brainstorming tool, can be adapted for church or personal use.

I. Bridges to Ministry

"Often Christians do not develop their ministry potential simply because they do not perceive they have anything special to offer."
—Russ Knight (p. 69).

This exercise will help you take inventory of potential "bridges to ministry" with children in poverty (p. 69). You may not think you have much that could make a difference—but remember the miracle of the five loaves and two fishes (John 6:5-14). This exercise asks you to prayerfully think through the two "fishes" you can offer to Jesus to multiply in service to Christ and others. Try to identify at least two responses for each category.

Appendix B

A. What do you have to offer?

1. *Material* resources you have that could be used to bless children (e.g., a salary, a home):

2. *Activities* you enjoy that you could share with children (e.g., playing sports, gardening):

3. *Skills* you have that you could use in service to children (e.g., graphic design, playing guitar):

4. *Connections* you have with people or institutions with special influence, skills, or resources to offer children in need and their families (e.g., employers, colleges):

B. Who is your neighbor?

1. *Children* you know who live in poverty (e.g., in your neighborhood or your child's school):

2. *Helpers* you know who could use support as they meet children's needs (e.g., social workers, health care professionals, teachers, caring individuals):

3. *Service organizations* you are interested in connecting with (e.g., Big Brothers/Big Sisters, pregnancy center):

4. *Issues* affecting children you are especially concerned about (e.g., health care, abuse):

C. How can you love your neighbor?

1. *Who are two specific children* with whom God is inviting you to share the love of Christ in word and deed?

2. *What are two specific concerns* related to poor children that you feel led to keep in prayer?

3. *What are two specific ways* you could use your resources, skills, interests, and connections to serve or advocate for poor children and their families (e.g., taking kids to a ball game, volunteering for an after-school program, campaigning for better health-care access, referring a job-seeking single mom to your employer)?

4. *What are two specific steps* you can take to connect with poor children—by making your home a place where they feel welcome (hospitality) and by entering into their world (solidarity)?

Share your responses with someone else in your neighborhood, congregation, or small group who can help encourage you to follow through on these ministry opportunities.

II. Church Ministry Planning

A. *Identify needs:* List concerns of children in poverty with particular relevance to your congregation and its community context. You may be drawn to a particular need (such as affordable housing, health care, or foster care) by the struggles of families in your neighborhood or congregation, by members' professional or personal experiences, or by a sense of calling. (Review the spectrum of concerns associated with child poverty in chapters 1 and 2 of this book.)

B. *Identify ministry possibilities:* In response to the needs you have identified, what specific ways could your congregation build on its experiences, skills, resources, and relationships to bring hope to children in poverty? Try to generate a range of ideas (see section III, "Brainstorming Ministry Ideas," p. 167) before selecting the top three possibilities. Identify options that are realistic next steps—start with doable but meaningful actions that can create momentum. Check whether other groups are already engaged in these areas.

C. *Turn ideas into action:* For each option above, plan (this may take some research):

■ **What** are the key decisions and action steps needed to make this ministry possible?

■ **How** will we obtain the resources and expertise to bring it about?

■ **Who** in our church or community group can take responsibility for the necessary steps?

■ **Who** can we connect with to multiply our impact (community leaders, local nonprofits and civic groups, foundations, other churches, national programs; see the organizations listed in Appendix A and the online study guide)?

■ **When** can we put these steps in action (timeline)?

D. *"Get our prayers straight"* (p. 25): How will you make prayer and love of God the bedrock of this ministry? What key Scriptures and spiritual disciplines can sustain your motivation through the challenges of service? See 2 Corinthians 8:3-5.

E. *Widen the circle:* With whom can you share your commitment to this vision, in order to expand the circle of those who are learning together about the needs of poor children, cultivating relationships with people in poverty, praying to see God's kingdom come (Matthew 6:10), and sharing accountability for action?

III. Brainstorming Ministry Ideas

Chapter 12 describes seven biblical pathways of action in response to poverty (p. 131–135). The table on the next page provides examples of child-centered ministries associated with each form of response (also see the suggested action steps in the online study guide). Use the blank column to note ideas related to needs, existing ministries, partnering resources, and potential ministry opportunities in your own context.

For more ideas on how churches can improve the lives of children, see the list developed by the United Methodist Church Bishops' Initiative on Children and Poverty, http://archives.umc.org/initiative/cfagc/check list.html.

Action responses to child poverty	Examples of ministry responses	Specific applications to our context
1. Practice hospitality and solidarity in our home and congregation	become foster parents; befriend at-risk youth; transport homeless families to church; include children from public housing in VBS	
2. Share resources with those in need	school supply kits; family homeless shelter; utility assistance; free immunizations	
3. Empower family self-sufficiency	job training; child care for parents in school; support for moms leaving welfare; resettlement assistance for immigrant/refugee families	
4. Invest in personal and community development	after-school tutoring; parenting class; playground installation; health care clinic	
5. Promote justice in government, business, and social institutions	organizing for living wages; school board involvement; advocacy for kids in the juvenile justice system; promoting anti-hunger legislation	
6. Create opportunities to break generational cycles of poverty	financial literacy for youth; scholarship incentives; teen pregnancy prevention; abuse counseling	
7. Share good news with the poor	church-based mentoring; art and music church camps; single parent support group; faith-based rite of passage programs	